SHEPHERD'S NOTES

Shepherd's Notes Titles Available

SHEPHERD'S NOTES COMMENTARY SERIES

Old Testament

9-780-805-490-282 Genesis
9-780-805-490-565 Exodus
9-780-805-490-695 Leviticus, Numbers
9-780-805-490-275 Deuteronomy
9-780-805-490-589 Joshua, Judges
9-780-805-490-572 Ruth, Esther
9-780-805-490-633 1 & 2 Samuel
9-780-805-490-077 1 & 2 Kings
9-780-805-490-649 1 & 2 Chronicles
9-780-805-491-944 Ezra, Nehemiah
9-780-805-490-060 Job
9-780-805-493-399 Psalms 1-50

9-780-805-493-405 Psalms 51-100
9-780-805-493-412 Psalms 101-150
9-780-805-490-169 Proverbs
9-780-805-490-596 Ecclesiastes, Song of Solomon
9-780-805-491-975 Isaiah
9-780-805-490-701 Jeremiah, Lamentations
9-780-805-490-787 Ezekiel
9-780-805-490-152 Daniel
9-780-805-493-269 Hosea, Obadiah
9-780-805-493-344 Jonah, Zephaniah
9-780-805-490-657 Haggai, Malachi

New Testament

9-781-558-196-889 Matthew
9-780-805-490-718 Mark
9-780-805-490-046 Luke
9-781-558-196-933 John
9-781-558-196-919 Acts
9-780-805-490-053 Romans
9-780-805-493-252 1 Corinthians
9-780-805-493-351 2 Corinthians
9-781-558-196-902 Galatians
9-780-805-493-276 Ephesians

9-781-558-196-896 Philippians, Colossians, Philemon
9-780-805-490-008 1 & 2 Thessalonians
9-781-558-196-926 1 & 2 Timothy, Titus
9-780-805-493-368 Hebrews
9-780-805-490-183 James
9-780-805-490-190 1 & 2 Peter & Jude
9-780-805-492-149 1, 2 & 3 John
9-780-805-490-176 Revelation

SHEPHERD'S NOTES CHRISTIAN CLASSICS

9-780-805-493-474 *Mere Christianity*, C. S. Lewis
9-780-805-493-535 *The Problem of Pain/ A Grief Observed*, C. S. Lewis
9-780-805-491-999 *The Confessions*, Augustine
9-780-805-492-002 *Calvin's Institutes*
9-780-805-493-948 *Miracles*, C. S. Lewis

9-780-805-491-968 *Lectures to My Students*, Charles Haddon Spurgeon
9-780-805-492-200 *The Writings of Justin Martyr*
9-780-805-493-450 *The City of God*, Augustine
9-780-805-491-982 *The Cost of Discipleship*, Bonhoeffer

SHEPHERD'S NOTES — BIBLE SUMMARY SERIES

9-780-805-493-771 Old Testament
9-780-805-493-788 New Testament

9-780-805-493-849 Life & Teachings of Jesus
9-780-805-493-856 Life & Letters of Paul

SHEPHERD'S NOTES

When you need a guide through the Scriptures

Daniel

HOLMAN
REFERENCE

NASHVILLE, TENNESSEE

978-0-8054-9015-2

Dewey Decimal Classification: 224.5
Subject Heading: BIBLE. O.T. DANIEL
Library of Congress Card Catalog Number: 97–37019

Library of Congress Cataloging-in-Publication Data
Daniel / Stephen Miller, author
      p. cm. — (Shepherd's notes)
      Includes bibliographical references.
      ISBN 978-0–8054–9015–2
      1. Bible. O.T. Daniel—Study and teaching.   I. Miller, Stephen R., 1949–
II. Series
BS1555.5.D36 1998
224'.507—dc21

                                97–37019
                                   CIP

21 22 23 24 25 26   19 18 17 16 15

Contents

Dear Reader:

Shepherd's Notes are designed to give you a quick, step-by-step overview of every book of the Bible. They are not meant to be substitutes for the biblical text; rather, they are study guides intended to help you explore the wisdom of Scripture in personal or group study and to apply that wisdom successfully in your own life.

Shepherd's Notes guide you through the main themes of each book of the Bible and illuminate fascinating details through appropriate commentary and reference notes. Historical and cultural background information brings the Bible into sharper focus.

Six different icons, used throughout the series, call your attention to historical-cultural information, Old Testament and New Testament references, word pictures, unit summaries, and personal application for everyday life.

Whether you are a novice or a veteran at Bible study, I believe you will find *Shepherd's Notes* a resource that will take you to a new level in your mining and applying the riches of Scripture.

In Him,

David R. Shepherd
Editor-in-Chief

HOW TO USE THIS BOOK

DESIGNED FOR THE BUSY USER

Shepherd's Notes for Daniel is designed to provide an easy-to-use tool for getting a quick handle on this Bible book's important features and for gaining an understanding of its message. Information available in more difficult-to-use reference works has been incorporated into the *Shepherd's Notes* format. This brings you the benefits of many advanced and expensive works packed into one small volume.

Shepherd's Notes are for laymen, pastors, teachers, small-group leaders and participants, as well as the classroom student. Enrich your personal study or quiet time. Shorten your class or small-group preparation time as you gain valuable insights into the truths of God's Word that you can pass along to your students or group members.

DESIGNED FOR QUICK ACCESS

Bible students with time constraints will especially appreciate the timesaving features built into the *Shepherd's Notes*. All features are intended to aid a quick and concise encounter with the heart of the message.

Concise Commentary. Daniel is one of the best-loved books in all the Bible. It combines two major forms of literature: narrative and prophecy. Portions of Daniel are some of the earliest material from the Bible that children come to know. The prophetic portions of Daniel are indispensable for beginning to understand The Revelation in the New Testament. Short sections enable you to grasp quickly the essentials of both the narrative and the prophetic portions of this important book and to see the importance of the book for God's people today.

Outlined Text. A comprehensive outline covers the entire text of Daniel. This is a valuable feature for following the flow of the book, allowing for a quick, easy way to locate a particular passage.

Shepherd's Notes. These summary statements appear at the close of every key section of the narrative. While functioning in part as a quick summary, they also deliver the essence of the message presented in the sections which they cover.

Icons. Various icons in the margin highlight recurring themes in Daniel and aid in selective searching or tracing of those themes.

Sidebars and Charts. These specially selected features provide additional background information to your study or preparation. These include definitions as well as cultural, historical, and biblical insights.

Maps. These are placed at appropriate places in the book to aid your understanding and study of a text or passage.

Questions to Guide Your Study. These thought-provoking questions and discussion starters are designed to encourage interaction with the truth and principles of God's Word.

DESIGNED TO WORK FOR YOU

Personal Study. Using *Shepherd's Notes* with a passage of Scripture can enlighten your study and take it to a new level. At your fingertips is information that would require searching several volumes to find. In addition, many points of application occur throughout the volume, contributing to personal growth.

Teaching. Outlines frame the text of Daniel, providing a logical presentation of the message. Capsule thoughts desginated as "Shepherd's Notes" provide summary statements for presenting the essence of key points and events. Application icons point out personal application of this message, and Historical Context icons indicate where background information is supplied.

Group Study. *Shepherd's Notes* can be an excellent companion volume to use for gaining a quick but accurate understanding of the message of a Bible book. Each group member can benefit by having his or her own copy. The *Note's* format accommodates the study of or the tracing of the major themes in Daniel. Leaders may use its flexible features to prepare for group sessions or use them during group sessions. Questions to guide your study can spark discussion of Daniel's key points and truths.

LIST OF MARGIN ICONS USED IN DANIEL

Shepherd's Notes. Placed at the end of each section, a capsule statement that provides the reader with the essence of the message of that section.

Old Testament Reference. Used when the writer refers to Old Testament Scripture passages that are related or have a bearing on the passage's understanding or interpretation.

New Testament Reference. Used when the writer refers to New Testament passages that are related to or have a bearing on the passage's understanding or interpretation.

Historical Background. To indicate historical, cultural, geographical, or biographical information that sheds light on the understanding or interpretation of a passage.

Personal Application. Used when the text provides a personal or universal application of truth.

Word Picture. Indicates that the meaning of a specific word or phrase is illustrated so as to shed light on it.

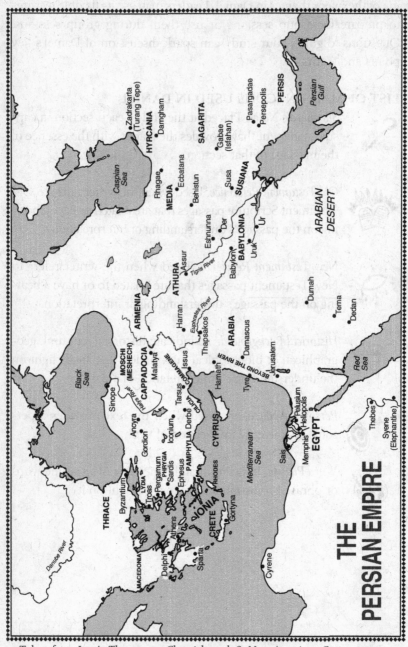

THE PERSIAN EMPIRE

Taken from Jay A. Thompson, *Chronicles* vol. 9, New American Commentary
(Nashville, Tenn.: Broadman & Holman Publishers), p. 20.

The Book of Daniel contains some of the most well-known stories in the Bible, and for that matter, in all of literature. Who has not heard about Daniel in the lions' den, the fiery furnace episode, and the handwriting on the wall?

Born about 620 B.C., Daniel lived in the small country of Judah. In 605 B.C. King Nebuchadnezzar took him as a captive to Babylon where he lived the remainder of his life. He probably died about 535 B.C.

According to the claims of the prophecy and Christian and Jewish tradition, Daniel composed the work that bears his name in the sixth century B.C. Though some have suggested a much later date for the book (second century B.C.) and questioned its historicity, Jesus Himself (see Matt. 24:15; 26:64; Mark 13:14; 14:62; Luke 22:69) and the New Testament writers (see Heb. 11:33–34) seem to confirm the traditional view.

Even though Daniel penned his prophecy over twenty-five centuries ago, its pages are filled with timeless truths that are just as relevant to modern believers as they were to those who first heard them.

Six narratives (chaps. 1–6) and four visions (chaps. 7–12) make up the contents of the prophecy. In the visions we find a type of literature called "apocalyptic" that frequently employs signs and symbols to convey its message. Apocalypse literally means "revelation," and the apocalyptic material in Daniel reveals insights concerning God and the future.

Judah's Captivity Predicted

Through His prophets, God had predicted long in advance the events described in this chapter. Over one hundred years before, Isaiah specifically warned Hezekiah that much of Judah's wealth and some members of the royal family would be taken to Babylon (see Isa. 39:5–7; cp. Isa. 48:20). Jeremiah also prophesied that the nation would fall to Babylon (see Jer. 20:4; 29:20–21).

"Lord"

The Hebrew word translated "Lord" in verse 2 is not *Yahweh* (represented in most translations by "LORD") but *Adonay*, "owner, ruler, or sovereign." Daniel's selection of this title emphasized the sovereignty of his God, the dominant theme of the book.

I. DANIEL'S IDENTITY AND CHARACTER (1:1–21)

In the first chapter of the book, the reader is provided information concerning Daniel's identity, his circumstances, his character, and how he rose to his position of responsibility in Babylon.

1. The Historical Setting (1:1–2)

Daniel reported that the Babylonians invaded Judah "in the third year of the reign of Jehoiakim" (609–598 B.C.). Nebuchadnezzar attacked Palestine after the battle of Carchemish (May-June 605 B.C.) and took Daniel and his three friends captive some time in the summer of that year.

Kings of Judah Reigning during Daniel's Lifetime

Josiah	640–609 B.C.
Jehoahaz	609 B.C.
Jehoiakim	609–597 B.C.
Jehoiachin	598–597 B.C.
Zedekiah	597–586 B.C.

God "delivered" Jehoiakim and the people of Jerusalem into Nebuchadnezzar's hand because of their sins (see 2 Chron. 36:5–6). For hundreds of years the Lord had warned His wayward people to repent or face judgment, but they had not listened to His servants, the prophets (see 9:6).

The Babylonians took with them "some of the articles from the temple of God," including the gold and silver cups and utensils, used in the Temple ceremonies in Jerusalem. These objects were seized because of their value as treasure (gold and silver) and as trophies of war. Nebuchadnezzar placed them in the temple of Marduk (Bel), the chief god of Babylon. About sixty-six years later, Belshazzar would bring these vessels into his feast and desecrate them (see Dan. 5:2–4).

"In Babylonia" is literally "to the land of Shinar." Shinar, the site of the tower of Babel (Gen. 11:1–9), was used elsewhere in the Old Testament as a designation for Babylon (see Isa. 11:11; Zech. 5:11). The name became associated with wickedness and rebellion against God. The righteous could expect opposition in Shinar.

"God"

In the original text, Daniel prefixed the article to the name, "God" (v. 2). This is a deliberate device that occurs throughout the book. It indicates that Daniel's God was not just one among the many in the Babylonian pantheon; but He was *the* God, that is, the one and only real God.

■ *Even in one of Judah's darkest hours, Daniel*
■ *saw the sovereign hand of God at work.*
■ *Surrender to the Babylonian armies*
■ *occurred not because Judah's God was*
■ *weak, but it was permitted as a judgment*
■ *because of the nation's sin. This passage*
■ *assures us that our God is in control even in*
■ *the worst circumstances.*

2. Introduction to Daniel and His Friends (1:3–7)

(1) Social Status (1:3)

Nebuchadnezzar ordered Ashpenaz, the leader of his "court officials" ("eunuchs," KJV), to take captives of some of the royal family and nobility of Judah. Daniel and his friends were probably

Nebuchadnezzar, King of Babylon

Nebuchadnezzar (605–562 B.C.) was the greatest ruler of the Neo-Babylonian Empire and one of the most competent monarchs of ancient times. He brought Babylon to the zenith of its economic affluence and political power. With his death in 562 B.C., the glory of Babylon immediately began to fade, and within twenty-three years the empire had collapsed. Nebuchadnezzar played a large part in biblical history.

members of both classes. The Hebrew word translated "court officials" could refer to a literal eunuch (see Isa. 56:3), but the term was also employed in a general sense to designate any official (see Gen. 37:36). Nebuchadnezzar had a policy of taking the intelligentsia and artisans from conquered territories for service in his kingdom. Being members of the royalty and leading families of the vanquished nation, these Jewish captives also would deter rebellion against Babylon lest they be harmed.

(2) Qualifications (1:4a)

The trainees had to be a certain age, probably about fourteen based on common Persian practice. Nebuchadnezzar wanted boys at a "teachable age" so they would be able and willing to learn new things. Daniel and his friends were also required to be in good physical health and to have a pleasing appearance. Intelligence was of the utmost importance since these young men would eventually serve as advisers to the king. Most likely, the expressions, "showing aptitude for every kind of learning, well informed, quick to understand," are cumulative and do not indicate distinct mental functions. "Qualified to serve in the king's palace" means that they possessed the social skills for serving in the royal court.

(3) Privileged Status (1:4b–5)

Daniel and his friends received a privileged education, a privileged diet ("from the king's table," and an opportunity to achieve a privileged position in the king's court. Their training period continued "for three years" (similar to Persian practice) and was intended to prepare the young men to serve the king in some capacity.

(4) Names (1:6–7)

The names of the Jewish captives were Daniel ("God is my judge"), Hananiah ("The Lord is gracious"), Mishael ("Who is what God is?"), and Azariah ("The Lord will help"). The Babylonians assigned the young men names indigenous to their new country, a common practice (see Gen. 41:45; Esther 2:7). These names were: Daniel=Belteshazzar ("Protect his life!" with the name of a pagan god implied, probably Marduk); Hananiah=Shadrach ("command of Aku," the moon god); Mishael=Meshach ("Who is what Aku is?"); Azariah=Abednego ("servant of Nebo," the second ranking god in the Babylonian pantheon). In each case the Hebrew appellation contained a reference to the true God, whereas its Babylonian counterpart alluded to a pagan deity. Some have suggested that this name change was an attempt to convert the Hebrews to paganism. If so, the plan did not succeed.

The Language and Literature of the Babylonians

The "language" of Babylon was a form of Akkadian known as Neo-Babylonian. Akkadian was written in wedge-shaped characters called cuneiform, commonly engraved on clay tablets. Archaeologists have uncovered thousands of these texts. Babylon was the learning center of the day and had acquired the remarkable library left by the Assyrian ruler, Ashurbanipal (669–626 B.C.). Its "literature" was extensive and included historical, legal, economic, mathematical, and religious texts.

■ *Daniel and his fellow captives from Judah*
■ *were outstanding young people. They had*
■ *been snatched from their homes, brought to a*
■ *strange land, given new names, and intro-*
■ *duced to new customs and a new language. In*
■ *spite of the trauma they must have experi-*
■ *enced, God had an exciting adventure and a*
■ *grand purpose for them in Babylon.*

3. The Moral Test (1:8–16)

(1) Daniel's Decision (1:8)

Daniel "resolved not to defile himself" with the king's food and wine for at least two reasons. First, some of the foods served at the royal court (for example, pork and horseflesh) would have

"Babylonians"

"Babylonians" (v. 4) is a translation of a Hebrew word often rendered "Chaldeans." In the Book of Daniel this term sometimes refers to a group of wise men (2:2, 4, 5, 10; 3:8; 4:7; 5:7, 11) and at other times is a general designation for the Babylonian people (cf. 1:4; 5:30; 9:1). The name was derived from the Semitic tribes who migrated to Babylonia from the Syrian desert and came to rule the country. Since the wise men were key leaders in Babylon, they were usually appointed from the ruling class, the ethnic Chaldeans. Thus the name came to designate the wise men as well.

Daniel's Moral Integrity

Daniel's refusal to eat the king's food was based on his deep religious convictions. He desired to remain true to God even though this decision could have cost him dearly. Believers today face moral tests and should follow the example of Daniel and his friends.

been unclean according to the Jewish dietary laws (see Lev. 11:1–47; Deut. 14:3–21). Second, a portion of the meat and wine was (at least on occasions if not always) offered sacrificially to the Babylonian gods before being served to the king's court and was therefore associated with idolatrous worship. Early Christians faced a similar dilemma (1 Cor. 10:25–28).

Daniel's request for an alternative diet was courageous for a number of reasons. (1) To refuse the royal diet could have been taken as an insult to the king and as an act of direct disobedience to Nebuchadnezzar's orders. Daniel could have been executed. (2) Pressure from Daniel's peers most certainly made the decision difficult. Everyone else was doing it. (3) Such unorthodox behavior could have jeopardized chances for advancement. (4) The quality of food would have been attractive. (5) Their new location may have tempted them to be unfaithful. Judah was nine hundred miles away; parents and friends would never know if they kept God's laws or not. Yet Daniel and his friends were aware that God would know. (6) They could have argued that, since God had not protected them from captivity, they did not have to be careful to obey His commands.

(2) Ashpenaz's Response (1:9–10)

The Lord "caused" Ashpenaz to have a favorable attitude toward Daniel (v. 9), demonstrating that Israel's God was even able to direct the hearts of the captors to accomplish His sovereign will (see Prov. 21:1). However, Ashpenaz feared that if these young men were not well taken care of he could lose not only his job but also his head!

(3) Daniel's Proposal (1:11–14)

Daniel asked the "guard" (a subordinate of Ashpenaz) if he and his friends might have an alternative diet for a ten-day period. The guard could then judge their physical condition after the test had been completed.

By this request, Daniel was not suggesting that eating meat was wrong (cp. Dan. 10:2–3), for a meat diet was permitted and in some instances even commanded in the Law (for example, in the case of the Passover lamb and other sacrifices).

The Hebrew word translated "vegetables" would also include fruits, grains, and bread. Daniel's diet was similar to many so-called health food diets today.

(4) The Outcome (1:15–16)

At the end of this period, the young men looked "healthier" and "better nourished" than the other youths who were eating the king's rich food (v. 15). So the overseer allowed Daniel and his friends to continue their new diet (v. 16). Nutritional experts today advocate a diet of mostly fruits and vegetables for optimum health. It is, therefore, no surprise that Daniel and his friends looked visibly healthier after following this menu, even for only ten days.

Opposition Expected

Believers today may expect opposition in an unrighteous world—our Babylon.

- *Daniel and his friends took a courageous*
- *stand for God, even though the decision could*
- *possibly have cost their lives.*

4. God's Blessings on Daniel and His Friends (1:17–21)

(1) God's Gifts (1:17)

God bestowed gifts on these young men for their faithfulness. All abilities and gifts ultimately come from the Lord who is the source of all blessings (James 1:17). Each of the four youths received the gift of keen intellectual

Dreams and Visions

Believers often wonder if God still speaks through dreams and visions today since this was a method of revelation during the biblical era. Dream and vision revelation would seem to be unnecessary in light of the fact that both the Old and New Testament records have now been completed. However, even if one believes that this is still a valid means of revelation, certainly no dream should be accepted as from God that contradicts revelation already imparted to the church through the Scriptures.

The word rendered, "magician" (v. 20), literally means "engraver" or "writer." Religious scribes recorded and preserved the materials used in the Babylonian religious activities. "Enchanters" (KJV "astrologers"; NASB "conjurers") employed magic spells and incantations to attempt communication with the spirit world.

ability, but Daniel had a special gift, not possessed by the others. The young prophet was miraculously endowed with a gift highly prized in that day, especially in Babylon—the ability to "understand" all kinds of "visions and dreams." This statement prepares the reader for the dreams and visions that follow later in the book.

(2) Favor before the Babylonian Court (1:18–20)

At the end of the three-year training period, Nebuchadnezzar interviewed Daniel and his friends and was far more impressed ("ten times better," v. 20) with them than with any of the others. Then they received positions of leadership in Nebuchadnezzar's administration.;

NAMES FOR WISE MEN IN THE BOOK OF DANIEL

Magician(s)	1:20; 2:2, 10, 27; 4:7, 9; 5:11
Enchanter(s)	1:20; 2:2, 10, 27; 4:7; 5:7, 11, 15
Sorcerers	2:2
Astrologer(s) [traditionally Chaldean(s)]	2:2, 4, 5, 10; 3:8; 4:7; 5:7, 11
Diviner(s)	2:27; 4:7; 5:7, 11
Wise Man/Men	2:12, 13, 14, 18, 24, 48; 4:6, 18; 5:7, 8, 15

(3) Long Life to Daniel (1:21)

Daniel was also blessed by the Lord with a long life, probably about eighty-five or ninety years (ca. 620–535 B.C.). The prophet did not die in the first year of King Cyrus, as the book later makes clear (see Dan. 6:1–2). Apparently the point of this verse is that Daniel lived throughout the entire Neo-Babylonian period (the exile) and continued into the reign of Cyrus (when the Jews were released from captivity), thus outliving his Babylonian masters.

■ *Believers are shown that those who are faith-*
■ *ful to God will reap divine blessings. Yet the*
■ *author did not mean to teach that believers*
■ *are always (as here) granted worldly success*
■ *as he makes abundantly clear in subsequent*
■ *passages (see Dan. 3:18; 7:25; 8:24). Faith-*
■ *fulness is invariably rewarded, but the*
■ *reward may be in the next life.*

QUESTIONS TO GUIDE YOUR STUDY

1. How is the theme of the Book of Daniel—God's sovereignty—exemplified in this chapter?
2. What does fulfilled prophecy demonstrate concerning the character and power of God?
3. What do the Hebrew and Babylonian names of the young men have in common? What may have been the motives in assigning the Hebrews these particular names?
4. Why did Daniel and his friends resolve not to eat the king's food? What factors made this a courageous decision?
5. Do you think that God always rewards righteousness? When?

Modern Magic

With the rise of certain religious movements, communicating with the spirit world through mediums or channels (called witches and sorcerers in the Bible) and delving into magic is again becoming popular. These activities are severely condemned in Scripture (see Exod. 22:18; Lev. 19:26; 1 Sam. 15:23; 28:3), and Christians should avoid all such practices.

The Christian and Political Office

There is a message in this story concerning the believer's participation in the political arena. Daniel exemplified the propriety of active service in governmental affairs under divine leadership.

II. NEBUCHADNEZZAR'S DREAM (2:1–49)

Nebuchadnezzar's first dream was imparted early in Daniel's experience in Babylon. The dream is significant because it provides a history of the world through four successive Gentile empires. During the final phase of the fourth empire, all earthly dominions will be destroyed, and the eternal kingdom of God will be established.

1. The Circumstances of the Dream (2:1)

Nebuchadnezzar had a disturbing dream in his "second year" (603–602 B.C.). Daniel was probably still a teenager. He was hardly the old prophet with the long white beard that most people imagine when reading this story. Ancient peoples believed that dreams were messages from the gods, and Nebuchadnezzar apparently feared that the strange revelation contained an ominous message for him.

Astrology

Astrology is quite popular today with many people professing to believe in its power, but it is not a new phenomenon. The practice may be traced even beyond Daniel's Babylon to earliest antiquity. That the movements of flaming spheres called stars and planets consisting of dirt and rock could determine a person's destiny is certainly ludicrous.

■ *The superstitious king was extremely fright-*
■ *ened by a strange dream.*

2. The Futility of the Pagan Interpreters (2:2–13)

(1) The Interpreters Called (2:2–4)

Sorcery (also called "witchcraft"; see Nah. 3:4) was widespread in the ancient world and was severely denounced in the Old Testament (Exod. 22:18; Deut. 18:10; Isa. 47:9, 12; Jer. 27:9; Mal. 3:5). "Astrologers" is a translation of a Hebrew word usually rendered "Chaldeans."

(The terms *magicians* and *enchanters* were discussed previously.)

The astrologers assured the king that if he would tell them the dream, they would interpret it (v. 4). The NIV translation gives the impression that the astrologers spoke to the king in the Aramaic language, but the phrase "in Aramaic" probably should be understood as a parenthetical notation placed in the text to mark the change in the written language. At this point in the book until the end of chapter 7, the language is not Hebrew but Aramaic.

(2) The Impossible Demand (2:5–9)

The KJV text indicates that the king had forgotten the dream, but most modern translations understand the passage similarly to NIV, "This is what I have firmly decided" (v. 5). The wise men understood fully that Nebuchadnezzar had not forgotten the dream because they continued to plead with him to reveal it. Nebuchadnezzar evidently refused to divulge the dream because he knew that his astrologers would offer an interpretation, but he would have no way to be certain that it was correct. However, if the wise men could tell the king the dream he did know, then he would also believe that they could accurately make known to him the interpretation, which he did not know.

Failure to fulfill the king's demand carried a severe penalty. The wise men would be dismembered either by being hacked to pieces or by being pulled apart, and their houses would be "turned into piles of rubble." Dismemberment of enemies was a practice widespread throughout the ancient world. On the other hand, if they interpreted the dream, they would receive "gifts and rewards and great honor" (v. 6).

Daniel's Two Languages

An unusual feature of the Book of Daniel is that roughly half is written in Hebrew (1:1–2:4a; 8:1–12:13) and half in Aramaic (2:4b–7:28). The most logical explanation is that Daniel recorded material that concerned the Gentile world in Aramaic (the world language of the day) but wrote those portions that particularly related to the Jews in their native Hebrew.

Dream Interpretation in Babylon

The Babylonian wise men were skilled in interpreting dreams and had manuals that explained the various dream symbols. Such explanations would not have been reliable but would have satisfied ignorant people. Archaeologists have discovered samples of these dream manuals.

Apparently Nebuchadnezzar did not hesitate to dispose of his wise men because he felt they were unable to fulfill their duties.

(3) The Admitted Inability (2:10–11)

The astrologers replied that no person on earth could fulfill the king's request, and they accused Nebuchadnezzar of being unreasonable. Only the gods, they declared, possessed such knowledge. This was a striking admission, for if only the gods knew the dream, whoever revealed the dream must be in touch with the gods.

(4) The Drastic Consequence (2:12–13)

Infuriated by the astrologers' blunt reply, the king ordered that they be assembled for a formal execution. This sentence of death included Daniel and his friends.

The Babylonian wise men were famous for sorcery, spells, and astrology, but their magic arts could not help them in their time of need (see Isa. 47:12–13). Neither could their false gods reveal the dream. Only the true God possesses wisdom, power, and salvation.

3. Daniel's Intervention (2:14–30)

(1) An Inquiry and Request (2:14–16)

When Daniel was informed of the matter, he went to Nebuchadnezzar and asked for time to interpret the dream. Evidently the request was granted because the prophet assured the king that his God could reveal the dream and its interpretation within a reasonable interval.

(2) A Revelation (2:17–19)

Daniel hurried home and explained the situation to his friends: Hananiah, Mishael, and Azariah (v. 17). Then he called the group to a time of prayer (v. 18). Here is a beautiful picture of four young men, possibly still in their teens, united in prayer. This was a life and death crisis, and they pleaded with God to have mercy on them and to preserve their lives. During the night the "mystery" (the dream and its interpretation) was revealed to Daniel in a vision. He praised the Lord for graciously granting their request (v. 19).

Lessons in Prayer

God's revelation was granted in response to Daniel's petition. Believers should not grow weary in prayer for God hears and answers their cries for help. These verses also illustrate the value of collective prayer. Special power seems to be promised when believers worship and pray together as a group (Matt. 18:19–20). Prayer should always include thanksgiving (Dan. 2:23).

Daniel's Names for God

Lord (1:2; 9:3, 4, 7, 9, 15, 16, 17, 19), sovereign, ruler

God (1:2, 9, 17, etc.), the powerful One

God of heaven (2:18, 19, 37, 44), the God in heaven

God of gods (2:47; 11:36), the greatest God

Lord of kings (2:47), the sovereign over the kings of the earth

Revealer of mysteries (2:29, 47), the omniscient One

Most High God (3:26; 4:2; 5:18, 21), the God above all

King of heaven (4:37), the ruler of heaven

Daniel's Names for God

Lord of heaven (5:23), the ruler of heaven

Living God (6:20, 26), the existing One

Ancient of Days (7:9, 13, 22), the eternal One

LORD (*Yahweh*) (9:2, 4, 8, 10, 13, 14, 20), the God who is

Prince of the host (8:11), ruler of the saints

(3) A Prayer (2:20–23)

These verses record one of the most beautiful praise prayers of the Bible. Daniel praised God for His "wisdom," demonstrated by His knowledge of the dream, and His great "power," manifested by the Lord's sovereignty over the events of human history.

The prayer concluded on a very personal note: "I," "my," "me," "we," "us," and the change from "he" to the more personal second person, "you," for God.

(4) The Appearance before the King (2:24–30)

Daniel found Arioch, the captain of the guard, and implored him not to kill the wise men because he was now prepared to interpret the dream. The young prophet was careful to give God all the glory. He acknowledged to the king that no human being could know the mystery, but "there is a God in heaven who reveals mysteries" (v. 28). That there is a God in heaven is the cardinal principle of the Bible.

Verse 28 also contains the first use of the term *divine*" ("soothsayer" KJV), a person who was purportedly able to "determine" another's fate. "Fortune teller" may well capture the idea. Nebuchadnezzar did not realize the sig-

"There is a God in heaven."

Circumstances may sometimes look impossible from an earthly viewpoint, but "there is a God in heaven" who can do all things. He can solve seemingly insoluble problems, supply needs, and provide strength for impossible tasks. God is there and cares for His children.

nificance of the dream, but God had granted him an amazing preview of future events ("days to come").

■ *Like Babylon's "diviners" of old, fortune-*
■ *tellers and psychics today fall short. They*
■ *claim to have the ability to forecast events*
■ *in advance, yet their predictions are seldom*
■ *accurate. True knowledge concerning spiri-*
■ *tual matters and the future come only from*
■ *God. He has revealed glimpses of the future*
■ *to His people through the Bible.*

4. The Dream Revealed (2:31–35)

At last the contents of the dream were revealed. What follows is one of the most amazing prophecies in the Bible.

(1) The Great Statue (2:31–33)

Nebuchadnezzar had seen an enormous statue in his dream. Consisting of metal, the statue reflected the light and was, therefore, "dazzling." The king was frightened by this colossus. The head of the statue was of gold, its chest and arms of silver, its belly and thighs of bronze, its legs of iron, and its feet were partly of iron and partly of baked clay. Baked clay would be brittle and weak.

(2) The Great Rock (2:34–35)

In the dream a rock was cut out ("of a mountain," v. 45) without human hands. Evidently, the rock was hurled by some force at the statue, striking it on its feet and breaking the iron and clay into pieces. Not only were the feet of iron and clay destroyed, but the entire statue (the bronze, silver, and gold) disintegrated into powder, and the wind blew away all traces of the

Brass or Bronze?

The KJV's rendering is "brass" in verse 32 (and elsewhere in Daniel), whereas the NIV and other modern versions translate "bronze." Bronze, an alloy of copper and tin, is probably a better translation, since the earliest known example of brass—an alloy of copper and zinc—is a Roman coin from about 20 B.C.

colossus. Then the rock that had destroyed the statue grew into a great mountain and filled the whole earth.

Several features of the rock would have impressed Nebuchadnezzar: (1) Its origin was supernatural, for it was cut out of the mountain without human hands; (2) the rock had extraordinary power, for it annihilated the statue; and (3) its scope was worldwide as symbolized by the fact that it grew into a huge mountain and filled the earth. In verses 44–45 Daniel identified this great rock as the coming kingdom of God, and its development into a huge mountain symbolized its universal dominion (see Isa. 2:2; Mic. 4:1).

■ *Someday the kingdom of God will come. It*
■ *will be universal.*

5. The Interpretation of the Dream (2:36–45)
(1) The Meaning of the Statue (2:36–43)
A panorama of four great Gentile empires, represented by the different materials in the statue, is set forth in the dream. Traditionally, these kingdoms have been identified as Babylon, Medo-Persia, Greece, and Rome. Some scholars have argued that the empires were Babylon, Media, Persia, and Greece. However, the traditional view conforms to historical reality.

THE BABYLONIAN EMPIRE (2:37–38)
Daniel identified Nebuchadnezzar and his Babylonian kingdom as the first empire. Frequently in Scripture the terms *king* and *kingdom* are employed interchangeably since the king was considered to be the embodiment of the kingdom.

For sixty-six years (605–539 B.C.) the Neo-Babylonian Empire ruled the Near East.

The Medo-Persian Empire (2:39a)

The next great power to appear on the world scene was the Medo-Persian Empire led by the dynamic Cyrus the Great (cp. 7:5; 8:20). This kingdom is symbolized by the silver chest and arms of the great statue, the two arms conceivably representing its two divisions.

Medo-Persian dominance continued for about two hundred years (539–331 B.C.).

This kingdom was "inferior" to Nebuchadnezzar's empire, and inferiority of each subsequent empire is expressed by the decreasing value of the metals. Possibly the inferiority in view is moral. Daniel may be suggesting that the sinfulness of the world will continue to increase until the culmination of history.

The Greek Empire (2:39b)

The bronze belly and thighs of the statue symbolized the Greek Empire (cp. 7:6; 8:5; 11:3–4). In 332 B.C. the armies of the great conqueror Alexander the Great marched against the Medo-Persian Empire and defeated it in a series of decisive battles.

The Greek Empire dominated the earth for almost two hundred years (331–146 B.C.).

Daniel declared that these kingdoms "rule over the whole earth," that is, over the civilized world of the day, and were not merely individual nations with limited influence. They were the great world empires of history.

The Roman Empire (2:40)

The image's legs of iron represent the empire that dominated the world after Greece—ancient Rome (v. 40). Five terms are utilized in this verse ("breaks," "smashes," "breaks to pieces," "crush," "break") to emphasize the tremendous power that this fourth kingdom would exert.

The Roman Empire dominated the world from the defeat of Carthage in 146 B.C. to the division of the east and west empires in A.D. 395—a period of approximately five hundred years. The last Roman emperor ruled in the west until A.D. 476, and the eastern division of the empire continued until A.D. 1453.

Some have suggested that the two iron legs of the statue represent the eastern and western divisions of the Roman Empire. Such an identification is not specifically expressed in the text and seems unlikely.

THE STATUE'S FEET AND TOES (2:41–43)

Among scholars who accept the traditional view, there is disagreement concerning the identification of the feet and toes of the statue. The key to understanding the passage rests on the interpretation of the rock that fills the earth. That the rock symbolizes the kingdom of God is specifically declared in the text (cp. 2:44–45); yet there is disagreement concerning the nature of this kingdom. If the kingdom refers to Christ's spiritual kingdom in the hearts of believers that commenced at His first coming, the feet and toes represent ancient Rome. If the dominion described in verse 44 alludes to Christ's personal, earthly kingdom to be inaugurated at His second coming, then the last part of the statue must depict an earthly empire existing immediately prior to Christ's return.

In verses 41–43 this fourth empire (whether ancient Rome or a future phase of Rome) is described as divided (a federation), powerful (iron), and mixed (consisting of strong and weak elements or nations). The "kings" of verse 44 have been identified as rulers symbolized by the ten toes of the statue who unite to form the last phase of the fourth empire and rule jointly until the time of Christ's return (see Dan. 7:24; Rev. 13:1; 17:12). Other scholars associate these "kings" in some manner with the ancient Roman period.

(2) The Meaning of the Great Rock
(2:44–45)

The climax of the dream revelation is the coming kingdom of God symbolized by the great rock (cp. v. 45; 7:13–14, 18, 27). This kingdom will be of divine origin, eternal ("never be destroyed"), triumphant ("crush"), and certain to come ("true" and "trustworthy").

- *In this present world of injustice, wars, and*
- *crime, it is comforting to know that someday*
- *the Messiah will appear and bring in the*
- *promised kingdom of God. Then the evils of*
- *this age will end. Indeed a day is coming*
- *when "the earth will be filled with the knowl-*
- *edge of the glory of the Lord, as the waters*
- *cover the sea" (Hab. 2:14).*

6. Nebuchadnezzar's Response (2:46–49)

The king was overwhelmed. He knew that Daniel had spoken the truth, so he fell on his face before the young Jewish captive (v. 46). Then Nebuchadnezzar gave honor to Daniel's God (v. 47). The Babylonian monarch was profoundly impressed, but he was not converted to the Jewish faith as his subsequent actions prove. As a polytheist he could always add another god to the deities he worshiped.

Daniel was rewarded with "a high position" and "many gifts" (v. 48). He did not forget his friends. At his request Nebuchadnezzar gave Shadrach, Meshach, and Abednego important political appointments (v. 49).

True Faith

Many people are like Nebuchadnezzar today. They know of the true God—many even believe in His miraculous powers—yet they have never come to know Him in a personal, experiential way. Yet such an experience is required, for Jesus Himself said, "Now this is eternal life: that they may know you, the only true God, and Jesus Christ, whom you have sent" (John 17:3).

- *Nebuchadnezzar and other Babylonians*
- *were impressed with the greatness of Daniel's*
- *God. The purpose of miracles is to bring*
- *glory to the Lord.*

QUESTIONS TO GUIDE YOUR STUDY

1. The Babylonian wise men could not reveal the dream or its meaning to the king. What are some examples of the failure of false religion in our modern world?
2. Why might Nebuchadnezzar have refused to reveal the dream to his wise men?
3. What are some of the elements in Daniel's prayer that should be in our prayers?
4. How did Daniel demonstrate his humility in this story?
5. What was the king's dream, and what did it mean? What relevance does the dream's message have for today?
6. What purpose for miracles may we observe in this story?

Names of the Three Hebrews Possibly Discovered in Ancient Babylonian Records

One scholar has presented a rather strong case for identifying the three Hebrews in this story with names found among more than fifty officials listed on a Babylonian text from the reign of Nebuchadnezzar. The names from the Babylonian list with their proposed Hebrew counterparts are: Hanunu=Hananiah (Shadrach), Ardi-Nabu=Abednego (Azariah), and Mushallim-Marduk= Mishael (Meshach).

DANIEL 3

III. THE TRIAL OF THE THREE HEBREWS (3:1–30)

The position of chapter 3 in the book, the probability that the king received the idea for the structure from the dream in chapter 2, and the likelihood that the image was constructed to test the loyalty of the king's officials to his new administration—all appear to support a time for this episode at the outset of Nebuchadnezzar's reign. Daniel's absence may be due to his responsibilities in Babylon (see Dan. 2:49), sickness, or some other unknown reason.

1. The Occasion (3:1–7)

(1) The Great Image (3:1)

King Nebuchadnezzar ordered that a huge statue be erected on a plain outside the city of Babylon. The enormous golden (overlay; cp. Exod. 39:38 with Exod. 30:3) statue was ninety feet high (roughly the height of a nine-story building) and nine feet wide. If the image was in human form, as most assume, these dimensions would seem quite disproportionate, even grotesque. The statue may have been similar to a totem pole, or more likely a base on which the statue stood made up much of the height. Dura has not been positively identified, but it must have been located somewhere near the city of Babylon. Gleaming in the bright sunlight, this golden colossus presented an imposing sight as it towered above the plain.

(2) The Dedication (3:2–3)

Nebuchadnezzar assembled his officials, who were to demonstrate their allegiance to the king and to Babylon's gods by bowing before the colossal statue. Seven different classes of officials are named, and it may be assumed that they were listed in order of importance, beginning with the most prominent. These are: (1) "the satraps" ("the princes," KJV), (2) "prefects" ("governors," KJV), (3) "governors" ("captains," KJV), (4) "advisers" ("counselors," NASB, NRSV; "judges," KJV), (5) "treasurers," (6) "judges" ("counsellors," KJV; "justices," NRSV) and (7) "magistrates" ("sheriffs," KJV). Other lesser important dignitaries are collectively specified as "all the other provincial officials."

Large Statues of Ancient Times

Large statues constructed by kings of ancient times were not uncommon. For example, the Great Sphinx in Egypt (240 ft. long by 66 ft. high) with its lion body and human head was constructed about 2500 B.C. and still casts its sightless glare over the desert sands. Rameses II and other pharaohs of Egypt built large statues of themselves and placed them throughout Egypt. Additional examples of huge statues are the Colossus of Rhodes (ca. 300 B.C.) that stood 105 feet tall and the great Statue of Zeus (40 ft. high) at Olympia, Greece (fifth century B.C.). According to the Greek historian Herodotus, there was a statue of Bel (Marduk) in Babylon (at least as early as the time of Cyrus) made of solid gold that stood eighteen feet high. With all of the wealth and manpower available to him, Nebuchadnezzar was fully able to construct the image described here.

(3) The Decree (3:4–6)

Many different nationalities were present, reflecting Nebuchadnezzar's policy of appointing native rulers to govern the provinces (e.g., Gedaliah, 2 Kings 25:22–25). These governmental officials were ordered to bow down and worship the golden image when the orchestra began to play. Musical instruments in the king's orchestra included the "horn" ("cornet," KJV), "flute" ("pipe," NRSV), "zither" ("lyre," NASB, NRSV; "harp," KJV), "lyre" ("trigon," NASB, NRSV; "sackbut," KJV), "harp" ("psaltery," NASB, KJV), and "pipes" ("bagpipe," NASB; "dulcimer," KJV; "drum," NRSV).

(4) The Worship (3:7)

Worship of a deity was clearly involved in this command to bow before the statue (see Dan. 3:28), and the image was probably in the likeness of Babylon's principal god, Marduk.

■ *Nebuchadnezzar ordered all his officials to*
■ *worship an idolatrous statue. Pressure is*
■ *often placed on believers to deny their God in*
■ *various ways.*

2. The Accusation (3:8–12)

(1) The Accusers (3:8)

In so vast a crowd the king evidently could not see that three men were left standing, and so "some astrologers" reported the fact. "Denounced" is literally "ate the pieces of," a phrase suggesting severe hatred and bitter language. "Chewed them out" might be a comparable English idiom, though not as harsh. The accusation probably reflected jealousy of the

Jews' success on the part of these wise men (see chap. 6).

(2) The Charges (3:9–12)

Three charges were brought against Shadrach, Meshach, and Abednego: they paid no attention to the king (and his commands), they did not serve the king's gods, and they refused to worship the golden statue that the king himself had set up.

- Shadrach, Meshach, and Abednego refused to
- bow before the great statue. Out of envy,
- some of their fellow wise men reported their
- actions to the king.

3. The Inquisition (3:13–18)

(1) The Question and the Offer (3:13–15)

In rage and disbelief, Nebuchadnezzar asked Shadrach, Meshach, and Abednego if the report of their disobedience was really "true." For some reason, Nebuchadnezzar granted these young men an opportunity to change their minds. Possibly he had grown fond of them, or perhaps he felt that it would be a pity to lose three capable men, especially since he had made a large investment of time and money in them. Then Nebuchadnezzar warned them that no god could rescue them if they refused to worship the image. This warning seems to reflect the king's previous experience with Israel's God (see chap. 2). The Lord had proven Himself powerful by revealing the dream, but even such a great God would not be able to protect His followers from death in the furnace.

Religious Persecution

The astrologers emphasized the fact that these disrespectful and treasonous men were "Jews" (v. 12; cp. v. 8). Since there appears to be no reason to point out their nationality, the designation seems to reflect a resentment toward the Jewish people and toward their religious practices which caused them to act so very differently from the rest of the world. God's people today are often persecuted when they take unpopular moral stands.

Trials and the Believer

God has the power to deliver believers from all problems and trials, but He often chooses not to do so. We may not always understand the purpose for trials (e.g., character building), but God asks us to trust Him—even when it is not easy. As Job who endured incredible suffering exclaimed, "Though he slay me, yet will I hope in him" (Job 13:15).

(2) The Courageous Reply (3:16–18)

The young men responded that they would not offer an apology for their stand. Although Shadrach, Meshach, and Abednego expressed confidence in their God's power to deliver them, they humbly accepted the fact that God does not always choose to intervene miraculously in human circumstances, even on behalf of His servants. The Hebrews believed that their God *could*—but not necessarily that He *would*—spare their lives.

Even if Shadrach, Meshach, and Abednego had to suffer a horrible, painful death in a burning oven, they declared that they would not forsake their God and worship idols. Belief in an afterlife is implied in their words (see Matt. 10:28).

Consequences of Uncontrolled Anger

The king was so angry that he ordered the soldiers to hurl the three Hebrews into the fire without proper preparation. His anger cost the lives of three innocent men. Our anger can have serious consequences as well.

- *Nebuchadnezzar gave the three Hebrews an opportunity to reconsider their decision.*
- *They expressed confidence in their God's ability to deliver them but realized that God might not choose to spare their lives. Nevertheless, they refused to worship the statue.*

4. The Sentence (3:19–23)

The bold words and unrepentant attitude of Shadrach, Meshach, and Abednego caused Nebuchadnezzar to become furious. He ordered that the furnace be heated "seven times hotter" than normal. "Seven times" is a proverbial expression (see Prov. 24:16; 26:16). Nebuchadnezzar may have selected some of his strongest soldiers to throw the Hebrews into the fire to prevent any intervention, whether human or divine. Shadrach, Meshach, and Abednego were tied up while still wearing their clothing and thrown into the flames. Their garments would have rapidly caught fire and engulfed the three in flames, a horrifying spectacle. The soldiers were forced to carry out the command so hurriedly that they did not have time to protect themselves from the fire, and the extreme heat killed them. "Fell into" the furnace suggests that the Hebrews were thrown in through an opening at the top.

- *The furious king ordered the unrepentant*
- *Hebrews thrown into the furnace. They were*
- *prepared to suffer martyrdom for their God.*

5. The Deliverance (3:24–27)

Nebuchadnezzar jumped to his feet in "amazement." The three Jews had been joined by a fourth man, and this one looked like "a son of the gods." Many scholars identify this person as an ordinary angel, but most likely He was a divine personage. "Son of the gods" ascribes deity to the being since an offspring of the gods partakes of the divine nature. God Himself was with His children in the middle of the fire.

The KJV renders this phrase, "the Son of God," an apparent allusion to the second person of the Trinity. Grammatically either the NIV or the KJV translation is possible. Since Nebuchadnezzar was polytheistic and had no conception of the Christian Trinity, the pagan king meant that the being in the fire was divine but did not go so far as to identify him as Jesus Christ. Nevertheless, this does not mean that the person in the fire was not Christ. Most likely He was since when God makes an appearance in the Old Testament, it is usually the second person of the Trinity.

Ancient Furnaces

Mesopotamian smelting furnaces resembled an old-fashioned glass milk bottle in shape. Ore to be smelted was inserted through the top, and wood and charcoal to furnish the heat were placed in the furnace through a smaller opening at ground level. The temperatures in these kilns could reach as high as 1000 degrees centigrade (about 1800 degrees Fahrenheit).

God's Presence in Trials

The three Hebrews experienced literally the promise, "When you walk through the fire, you will not be burned; the flames will not set you ablaze" (Isa. 43:2). When believers today go through fiery trials, God is with them as well.

Death by Burning

Jeremiah 29:22 records the fact that Nebuchadnezzar burned to death two men named Zedekiah and Ahab.

Death by burning in a "blazing furnace" was the awful penalty for disobeying the king's order. Nebuchadnezzar probably chose this means of punishment, not only because it was a horrifying way to die, but also because it was convenient. A huge kiln would necessarily have been available to smelt metal for the gold plating and for manufacturing the bricks to construct the base and possibly the inner parts of the statue itself.

Respect for Commitment to God

Even in today's world, unbelievers may not understand or appreciate Christian convictions, but usually they respect those who are willing to take a stand for their God.

Nebuchadnezzar came near the opening of the furnace and shouted for the Hebrews to come out and appear before him. The king was now convinced that the God of Israel was truly great, "the Most High God." Yet this faith was well within the scope of pagan, polytheistic religious concepts, for the king merely considered the Lord the great God among many. When the three came out of the fire, there was no evidence that they had been in the furnace. There was not even any "smell of fire on them." All were convinced that they had witnessed a miracle.

■ *The three Hebrews witnessed a great miracle*
■ *and had a personal encounter with God in*
■ *the flames. God was with them in their time*
■ *of need as He is with believers today.*

6. The Result (3:28–30)

Nebuchadnezzar praised the God of the Hebrews for such a great demonstration of power. "Angel" (lit., messenger) could denote an ordinary angel or God Himself (see Gen. 18:1–2, 10ff.). In this context, it refers to a divine being as the discussion at verse 25 shows. The pagan monarch expressed his admiration for these young men because of their willingness to suffer a horrible death in order to remain true to their God.

Nebuchadnezzar issued a decree forbidding all subjects throughout his kingdom from saying anything bad about Israel's God on penalty of death and destruction of their property (cp. 2:5). Such a command from the lips of a heathen king is astounding, but one must consider the circumstances—Nebuchadnezzar had just witnessed a miracle. This decree may also have been an attempt to appease the God of Israel, for the king may have feared that he was in danger of divine retaliation.

Shadrach, Meshach, and Abednego were not only honored by the king; but they also received rewards. Probably material rewards and respect among the people were involved as well as a job promotion. Thus, faithfulness in a dreadful trial resulted in great blessing for the three Jewish men.

- The result of the Hebrews' faithfulness and
- their miraculous deliverance was that the
- king gave glory to the true God, and the
- Hebrews were rewarded.

QUESTIONS TO GUIDE YOUR STUDY

1. What was the likely purpose of the great statue that Nebuchadnezzar set up on the plain of Dura?
2. Why did the king choose death in the furnace as punishment for refusing to bow before the image?
3. Did the Hebrews believe that their God had the power to deliver them from death in the furnace? Were they certain that God would deliver them? What kind of attitude did they exhibit in light of the possibilities?
4. Who was the fourth person in the flames?

An Encouragement to Faithfulness

The author of the epistle to the Hebrews inspired saints in his day by reminding them of past heroes of the faith. Those who had "quenched the fury of the flames" (Heb. 11:34) no doubt were the three Hebrews of Daniel 3. If the Lord could deliver the Hebrews from the furnace, He can see saints today through their fiery trials.

The Omnipotence of God

To be thrown into a furnace of blazing fire and to live is certainly extraordinary. Yet the angel Gabriel told Mary, "Nothing is impossible with God" (Luke 1:37), and the Lord Jesus Himself said, "With God all things are possible" (Matt. 19:26). Daniel 3 illustrates that God has sufficient power to protect His children.

....

IV. NEBUCHADNEZZAR'S SECOND DREAM: GOD'S JUDGMENT ON THE KING (4:1–37)

Daniel did not date the dream and subsequent events described here, but clues in the text point to the close of Nebuchadnezzar's reign. For example, his building operations seem to have been concluded (4:30), and there is peace throughout the empire (4:4). This chapter is unusual in a number of ways: (1) It contains some features similar to those of an epistle; (2) it is the only chapter in Scripture drafted under the authority of a pagan; (3) the chapter is written from Nebuchadnezzar's viewpoint; (4) there are doxologies at the beginning and end of the chapter; (5) a change from first (vv. 1–18, 19b–27) to third person (vv. 19a, 28–33) and then back to first person (vv. 34–37) occurs in the chapter. For the most part, the material written in the third person (except v. 19a) describes the king's madness, details to which the king would not have been a sane witness.

1. The King's Proclamation (4:1–3)

Nebuchadnezzar's universal audience is typical of Assyrian and Babylonian royal claims to rule the whole earth. The purpose of the letter was to declare the greatness and power of the "Most High God" that had been exhibited in the king's life. "It is my pleasure" shows that it was a true joy for Nebuchadnezzar to share what God had done for him.

Nebuchadnezzar praised the Lord for His greatness, power, and sovereignty. At last the king had come to realize that "the Most High God," not himself or the gods of Babylon, was sover-

Delighted to Tell of God's Goodness

Nebuchadnezzar was delighted to share his testimony with others. This should be the attitude of every believer. God has done something wonderful for us in salvation, and we should consider it a "pleasure" to share that experience with others.

eign. From the lips of a pagan monarch, these affirmations concerning Israel's God are truly incredible. Yet it is understandable, considering the many ways in which the Lord had demonstrated His reality and power to Nebuchadnezzar (recorded in chaps. 2–4) and the constant witness of Daniel in the court.

■ *Nebuchadnezzar had personally experienced*
■ *the greatness of Israel's God. He desired to*
■ *share his testimony with the world.*

2. The King's Dream (4:4–18)

(1) The Circumstances of the Dream (4:4–5)

The king was enjoying peace and prosperity on every hand. His opposition (including the Egyptians) had been subdued, and there was no serious threat to his authority. Suddenly, the king's carefree life was shattered by a strange dream that "terrified" the mighty Nebuchadnezzar.

(2) The Interpreter of the Dream (4:6–9)

As in previous instances, Babylon's wise men were unable to interpret the dream. Finally, Daniel appeared before the king. Daniel's qualification for interpreting dreams was that God ("the spirit of the holy gods") dwelt within him. This is the prerequisite for spiritual understanding today.

(3) The Contents of the Dream (4:10–17)

Nebuchadnezzar reported that he had seen an enormously tall tree in the middle of the "land" (NIV) or "earth" (KJV, NRSV). The context seems to demand, "earth," since Nebuchadnezzar's domain (symbolized by the tree) reached beyond the boundaries of his own "land." Evidently the tree was centrally located to denote its

"Messenger, a Holy One"

"Messenger" literally means "one who is awake." This title occurs only in this chapter (vv. 13, 17, and 23) in the Bible, although it appears in later Jewish literature as a designation for *angels*. The idea is that God's holy angels are awake and keeping watch over the activities of the human race.

Lycanthropy

"Lycanthropy" (lit., "wolf-man") originally referred to the delusion of believing oneself to be a wolf like creature (the primitive werewolf superstition was inspired by this malady) but today has come to be a general designation for this illness, regardless of the type of animal involved. Some historical figures who fell victim to the malady are King George III of England and Otto of Bavaria. Though rare, the disease occurs today and has been documented in psychological studies.

position of supreme importance in relation to the rest of the earth. The top of the tree touched the sky, and "it was visible to the ends of the earth." The tree was "beautiful," providing food and protection for the animals and birds.

An angel came down from heaven and commanded that the tree be cut down and stripped of its branches, leaves, and fruit. Yet its stump and roots were left standing in the middle of the grassy field, suggesting the possibility that the tree might grow again. A band or fence of iron and bronze was to be placed around the stump of the tree to protect it from destruction. This metal band was symbolic of the preservation of Nebuchadnezzar's life and kingdom (cp. vv. 23, 26). In the middle of verse 15 the description changes from a tree to that symbolized by the tree, a man. This man would live outdoors with the animals of the field where he would be exposed to the elements of nature.

He would actually believe himself to be an animal, a psychological condition known as lycanthropy. His illness would continue until "seven times" were completed. Most scholars, ancient and modern, have interpreted the seven times as seven years (see 7:25), though there are those who take the phrase to designate an unspecified period of time.

Heaven's decision to judge this man with insanity was made to demonstrate God's sovereignty "over the kingdoms of men." As a rebuke to Nebuchadnezzar's pride and to that of all earthly kings, God pointed out that at times He even allows the "lowliest of men" to reign.

(4) *The Request of the Dreamer* (4:18)
Once more the king expressed faith in his chief counselor's ability to interpret the dream

because he was aware of Daniel's special relationship with the spiritual world (cp. vv. 8, 9). Another reason for Nebuchadnezzar's confidence was that the prophet had interpreted a difficult dream for him on a previous occasion (see chap. 2).

■ *Nebuchadnezzar was basking in the glow of*
■ *his many accomplishments when he had a*
■ *frightening dream. The events described in*
■ *the dream were decreed so that all would*
■ *know that God rules over the affairs of the*
■ *human race.*

3. The Interpretation of the Dream (4:19–27)

(1) Daniel's Hesitation (4:19)

"Greatly perplexed" (NIV) would be better rendered "appalled" or "astounded." Daniel was not "perplexed" concerning the meaning of the dream, as the rest of the verse plainly shows; rather he was "astounded" by the horror of what he immediately knew the dream foretold. Thoughts of these coming events "terrified" (better, "alarmed") Daniel, not only because the prophet seemed genuinely to like and respect the Babylonian monarch but because of the effect this situation could have on the Jewish people. Nebuchadnezzar had evidently treated the Jews well throughout most of his reign. If he were deposed, there would be no guarantee of a like-minded ruler.

(2) The Dream Explained (4:20–26)

Daniel related that the great tree represented Nebuchadnezzar and his vast kingdom that had afforded prosperity and protection to the peoples of the earth. In the Old Testament, the tree figure is employed elsewhere to speak of human pride (see Isa. 2:12–13; 10:34; Ezek. 31:3–17). Many commentators have noted the similarity between the phrase "you, O king, are that tree!" and Nathan's words to David, "You are the man!" (2 Sam. 12:7).

Nebuchadnezzar was specifically named as the person who would behave like an animal. Because of his strange behavior, the king would "be driven away from people" and live with the "wild animals" (better, "animals of the field"). Nebuchadnezzar would imagine himself to be a bull or an ox.

This insane behavior would continue for seven years ("seven times") until the king repented of his pride and acknowledged that the Most High God was sovereign. Repentance was possible because with this particular malady many times a person might reason quite well in certain areas even though exhibiting animal characteristics. For example, in one modern study a man who believed himself to be a cat for a period of over thirteen years was gainfully employed.

Daniel offered the king a ray of hope by explaining that the stump and roots being spared meant that his kingdom would be restored on his repentance. During this period of mental incapacitation, Nebuchadnezzar's son, Amel-Marduk, apparently ruled the country so that the government continued to function normally.

(3) Daniel's Advice (4:27)

Daniel tactfully encouraged the king to repent of his sins and demonstrate his repentance by right living. By heeding the warning in this dream and performing good deeds, the monarch would prove that he acknowledged God's supremacy over him. Daniel seemed to hold out to the king the genuine possibility of foregoing this judgment, demonstrating God's willingness to forgive.

■ *The dream foretold God's judgment on Neb-*
■ *uchadnezzar. Daniel encouraged the king to*
■ *renounce his sins in order to avoid the com-*
■ *ing calamity. God is merciful and willing*
■ *to forgive.*

4. The Fulfillment of the Dream (4:28–36)

(1) *Nebuchadnezzar's Judgment (4:28–33)*

Regrettably, Nebuchadnezzar did not repent, and all of the horrible events foretold in the dream transpired. Twelve months later a great outburst of pride on the part of the Babylonian monarch became the catalyst for the dream's fulfillment.

Nebuchadnezzar was walking on the flat roof of his royal palace looking out over the magnificent city that he had built. He referred to the city as "the great Babylon" (see Rev. 14:8; 18:2), and indeed it was great. Babylon was one of the preeminent cities of history and during Nebuchadnezzar's reign was undoubtedly the most magnificent city on earth. Herodotus, the ancient Greek historian, visited the city about one hundred years after Nebuchadnezzar's time and was overwhelmed by its grandeur. Over two hundred years later, Alexander the Great (who died in Babylon) planned to make the city the headquarters for his vast empire.

Nebuchadnezzar failed to give God the glory for his achievements, and his heart was filled with

Salvation by Works?

Daniel's counsel to the king was not a "plan of salvation." Neither Nebuchadnezzar nor anyone else can be saved by works. Salvation involves a personal experience with the living God with right living naturally flowing out of a changed life. However, temporal judgment may be avoided by correct living.

God's Mercy

In His mercy God had graciously allowed Nebuchadnezzar a full year to repent of his sins, but the proud king did not do so. God is patient and loving. He does not take pleasure in judging people (cf. Ezek. 18:23, 32).

A Description of Ancient Babylon

Babylon was a rectangularly shaped city surrounded by a broad and deep moat and by an intricate system of double walls. Nebuchadnezzar added another defensive double-wall system east of the Euphrates River that ran the incredible distance of seventeen miles and was wide enough at the top for chariots to pass. The height of the walls are not known, but the Ishtar Gate was 40 feet high, and the walls would have approximated that size. A great ziggurat with its seven levels towered 288 feet into the air. Babylon also boasted the famous "hanging gardens" that the ancient Greeks considered one of the seven wonders of the world.

pride. The first person pronouns ("I," "my") are conspicuous in verse 30.

A voice from heaven pronounced judgment on him, and immediately the horrible sentence was carried out. Because of his bizarre animal-like behavior, Nebuchadnezzar "was driven away from people." He lived outdoors with the beasts, "ate grass like cattle," and was exposed to the weather. His hair became matted and coarse, and his nails grew long. How ironic that the king who had considered himself superior to other men now sank to a subhuman level!

(2) Nebuchadnezzar's Restoration (4:34–36)

Now the account reverts to first person, and Nebuchadnezzar continued his personal testimony. At the end of the seven years, the king raised his eyes toward heaven, an act of submission, surrender, and acknowledgment of his need for the Most High God. God observed Nebuchadnezzar's simple gesture of humility and repentance and graciously restored his "sanity." Then the king "praised" God as sovereign ("the Most High") and "honored" and "glorified" Him as the eternal One. Nebuchadnezzar had come to realize that his kingdom was temporal, but God's kingdom is eternal.

God's sovereignty is emphasized in verse 35. The "powers of heaven" may refer to the heavenly bodies (sun, moon, and stars), to the angelic forces (or armies) of heaven, or both. Since the phrase parallels the "peoples of the earth," probably the inhabitants of heaven are intended. Nebuchadnezzar related that in his latter years he received more power and honor than before his humiliating experience.

■ *Nebuchadnezzar did not repent and God's*
■ *judgment forewarned in the dream was ful-*
■ *filled. When the king repented, God in His*
■ *mercy restored Nebuchadnezzar to his posi-*
■ *tion of authority. The Lord demonstrated His*
■ *power over the greatest of earth's rulers.*

5. Conclusion (4:37)

Nebuchadnezzar concluded his testimony with an additional word of praise to "the King of heaven." In the latter part of the chapter's final verse, the moral of the story is stated, "And those who walk in pride he is able to humble."

Nebuchadnezzar certainly had an encounter with the living God, and his praise seems to have been sincere. Was his experience equivalent to salvation, or did it fall short of saving faith? Although scholars are divided over the question, it seems that the language of the text suggests that Nebuchadnezzar did have a saving encounter with the true God.

God's concern for persons in every part of the world may also be observed in this account. Even in pagan Babylon, there was a witness—spiritual light—to the power and reality of the Lord.

■ *Nebuchadnezzar praised the Lord for His*
■ *mercy and acknowledged that God was able*
■ *to humble the proud.*

The Danger of Pride

This episode illustrates the well-known proverb, "Pride goes before destruction, a haughty spirit before a fall" (Prov. 16:18). God hates pride and humbles those who will not acknowledge His sovereignty over them (James 4:6). Persons who walk in pride today discover that this cause-and-effect spiritual law continues to operate.

QUESTIONS TO GUIDE YOUR STUDY

1. What is unusual about this chapter?
2. What was Nebuchadnezzar's dream and what did it mean?
3. What is the name of the mental illness that afflicted Nebuchadnezzar? Are there instances of this illness today?
4. Why was Daniel silent when he heard the dream?
5. What great sin is rebuked in this chapter?

DANIEL 5

Historicity of Belshazzar

Until the last half of the nineteenth century, the name *Belshazzar* was unattested except for the Book of Daniel and works dependent on it, such as Baruch and Josephus. Since that time, abundant evidence has come to light that demonstrates not only that Belshazzar lived but also that he was indeed the son of, and coregent with, his father Nabonidus.

KINGS OF THE NEO-BABYLONIAN EMPIRE

Nabopolassar	625–605 B.C.
Nebuchadnezzar	605–562 B.C.
Amel-Marduk	562–560 B.C.
Neriglissar	560–556 B.C.
Labashi-Marduk	556 B.C.
Nabonidus	
Belshazzar (son of Nabonidus who served as coregent during most of his father's reign)	556–539 B.C.

V. BELSHAZZAR'S FEAST AND THE FALL OF BABYLON (5:1–31)

Nabonidus, the last king of Babylon, resided at Tema in Arabia (about five hundred miles south of Babylon) for most of his seventeen-year reign, apparently for religious reasons. During these long absences, it was Belshazzar, the crown prince, who ruled the empire.

Nebuchadnezzar is called Belshazzar's father six times (vv. 2, 13, 18, and three times in v. 11), and the king is designated as the son of Nebuchadnezzar once (v. 22). In the Semitic languages, "father" and "son" have a wide range of meanings. "Father" may refer to one's immediate father, grandfather, ancestor, or in the case of kings, a predecessor. Likewise, "son" may mean one's immediate offspring, grandson, descendant, or successor. Most likely Belshazzar was Nebuchadnezzar's grandson. Belshazzar's relationship with Nebuchadnezzar is emphasized because Belshazzar should have learned the lesson of humility and submission to Israel's God from the episode in the life of this great king.

Large feasts were not uncommon in ancient times. One Persian king fed fifteen thousand persons daily, and Alexander entertained ten thousand guests at a marriage festival. According to Esther 1:1–4, Xerxes I held a gathering for a large number of people that lasted 180 days. Belshazzar celebrated this feast on October 12, 539 B.C., about thirty years after the events recorded in chapter 4.

1. The Feast (5:1–4)

(1) Immorality (5:1)

Belshazzar hosted a huge "banquet for a thousand of his nobles."

It may safely be assumed that within a short period the king and his guests were well on their way to inebriation. With inhibitions relaxed, the affair probably degenerated into a drunken orgy.

Ancient Testimony Concerning Belshazzar's Feast

Both Herodotus and Xenophon (ancient Greek historians) testified that a banquet was in progress on the night Babylon fell.

The purpose of this feast is puzzling. Outside the city walls camped the Persian armies. The Babylonians had suffered a crushing defeat just days before at the hands of the Persians, and only the great city of Babylon remained unconquered. The situation appeared bleak. Under such circumstances, why would Belshazzar host a feast? Belshazzar may have observed this celebration to build morale, or this may have been a customary festival that simply happened to fall at this time.

Invincible Babylon

Babylon's walls seemed invincible, and the Euphrates River ran through the city so there was an ample water supply. The ancient Greek historian Xenophon reported that the city had been stocked with enough food to last for twenty years. Belshazzar probably believed that God Himself could not touch him within the massive walls of Babylon.

The Sin of Blasphemy

The sin of blasphemy is one of the worst sins that anyone can commit. It brings the judgment of God on an individual or nation. Jesus declared that the blasphemy of the Holy Spirit is the unpardonable sin (see Matt. 12:31). Blasphemous attacks on the person and law of God are not uncommon today, particularly by means of television and movies.

(2) Blasphemy (5:2–4)

Belshazzar, his judgment impaired by the wine, ordered the sacred vases from the temple at Jerusalem to be brought into his drunken orgy (cp. 1:2). Then he and his guests blasphemed Israel's God by filling these goblets with wine and drinking toasts to the pagan gods of Babylon. Daniel called the Babylonian idols gods of gold, silver, bronze, iron, wood, and stone because in his mind this was all the substance they had (see Ps. 115:4–7; 135:15–17).

In verses 22–24 Daniel indicated that the king's blasphemy was a deliberate act of defiance against the Lord's authority and power. Belshazzar knew that Israel's God had humbled Nebuchadnezzar; yet he willfully challenged this God to humble him. The arrogant king may also have heard of the Lord's predictions of Babylon's fall to Medo-Persia (see Dan. 8:1–4, 15–20; Isa. 44:28; 45:1).

■ *Drunkenness, immorality, pride, idolatry,*
■ *and blasphemy were some of the Belshaz-*
■ *zar's sins. These sins are prevalent today and*
■ *have serious consequences.*

2. The Handwriting on the Wall (5:5–6)

"Suddenly," at the height of Belshazzar's blasphemy, "the fingers of a human hand appeared" and began to write a message on the wall. Against the white "plaster" wall any writing (and the moving hand) would have stood out clearly. The message was also written near the "lampstand," rendering the script even more visible to all in the room. The arrogant king turned white as a ghost, and his knees began to knock.

■ *God sometimes reveals Himself in unusual*
■ *ways. Those who blaspheme God and His*
■ *law will inevitably regret it.*

3. The Wise Men of Babylon Called (5:7–9)

Belshazzar promised a threefold reward to any
of his wise men who could interpret the writing.
They would be clothed in purple, receive a
necklace of gold (both symbols of high rank),
and be promoted to "the third highest ruler in
the kingdom." "Third highest" implies two other
persons. The two persons who would outrank
the interpreter were Belshazzar and his father
Nabonidus. Daniel was cognizant of Nabonidus,
though he did not mention him by name. Even
for attractive prizes, Belshazzar's wise men were
unable to interpret the inscription on the wall.

THE INDECIPHERABLE MESSAGE

Although the message was written in a language
the wise men understood (Aramaic; cp. vv.
25–28), they could not read the message on the
wall. Perhaps the letters were written in an
unusual manner. Most likely the words themselves were understood, but they did not convey
any intelligible meaning.

■ *Once more we see that divine revelation is*
■ *only understood with illumination from God.*

4. Daniel Summoned (5:10–16)

The queen (v. 10) was not Belshazzar's wife, for
Daniel stated earlier that the wives of the king
were already present. Moreover, this woman

The Royal Throne Room

The very room where
Belshazzar's feast
took place may have
been discovered. Off
the largest of the royal
palace's five
courtyards was a
huge chamber (about
170 by 56 ft.) with
three entrances that
some archaeologists
have identified as the
throne room. The
room had a
background of dark
blue glazed bricks and
tall columns of yellow
glazed bricks topped
with bright blue Ionic
capitals. The roof was
constructed of cedar,
and the windowless
walls were
whitewashed.

displayed firsthand information concerning the affairs of Nebuchadnezzar that would not have been known by a younger wife of Belshazzar, and she apparently had observed Daniel's ministry in Nebuchadnezzar's court. Likely she was Belshazzar's mother. The queen reminded Belshazzar of Daniel and assured the king that the old prophet could explain the writing on the wall. Belshazzar informed Daniel concerning the situation and promised him the three-fold reward for interpreting the inscription.

"Though You Knew All This" (v. 22)

How could Belshazzar have been aware of Nebuchadnezzar's humiliation? Certainly the story would have been known, but historical evidence indicates that Belshazzar probably saw the events firsthand. Belshazzar served as chief officer during the administration of King Neriglissar in 560 B.C.. This means that the king was old enough to fill a high position in government only two years after Nebuchadnezzar's death (562 B.C.). Since Nabonidus was an official in Nebuchadnezzar's administration, Belshazzar would have lived in Babylon and personally observed the last years of the great king's reign.

■ *During this hour of crisis, the queen encour-*
■ *aged Belshazzar to seek wisdom from God's*
■ *prophet. People should seek spiritual guid-*
■ *ance from the true God.*

5. A Refusal and a Rebuke (5:17–24)

Daniel refused Belshazzar's gifts in order to alleviate any misconception that God's services could be bought and to avoid obligation to the king (cp. 2 Kings 5:15–16). Before interpreting the writing, Daniel reprimanded the king. He began by reminding Belshazzar of the consequences of pride in the life of Babylon's greatest king, Nebuchadnezzar, and concluded by condemning Belshazzar's blasphemous and deliberate defiance of the Most High God. Belshazzar refused to humble himself before God, although he knew all that had happened to Nebuchadnezzar. The wicked king praised his lifeless idols, but the living God who held his very life (lit., "breath") and all his "ways" (his life's course) in His hand, the king refused to honor (v. 23).

Thus, Daniel's rebuke is even more understandable. Belshazzar had seen what happened to Nebuchadnezzar with his own eyes, and yet he had defiantly refused to humble himself before the Most High God.

Daniel concluded his "sermon" by telling Belshazzar that it was because of his blasphemous, defiant actions that the hand was sent from the living God. The old prophet's words demonstrated great courage in the face of a monarch who held the power of life and death over him.

■ *Daniel demonstrated courage in rebuking*
■ *the wicked king for his pride and idolatry.*
■ *Belshazzar had acted foolishly by rejecting*
■ *the true God, especially after observing the*
■ *great Nebuchadnezzar's humiliating*
■ *experience.*

6. The Handwriting Explained (5:25–28)

Only four brief words were written on the palace wall—"mene, mene, tekel, parsin." "*Mene, mene*" ("numbered, numbered"; twice for emphasis) signified that God had numbered the days (see Ps. 90:12) of the king's reign and decreed that they would be brought to an end. Belshazzar's evil rule (and his life) would soon be over. "*Tekel*" ("weighed") meant that Belshazzar's wicked life had been weighed against God's moral law, and the king was found deficient in moral worth (see Job 31:6; Prov. 16:2; 21:2; 24:12). "*Peres*" ("divided") indicated that Belshazzar's kingdom would be divided by the conquering Medes and Persians.

Honoring the Wrong Gods

Belshazzar worshiped the lifeless idols of Babylon, but Daniel said that he "did not honor the God who holds in his hand your life and all your ways." So often today people honor the lifeless gods of this world and have no time for the living God, who literally holds their very breath in His hands.

"Peres"

Only the consonants were written in ancient Aramaic and Hebrew scripts. The word *peres* has the same consonants as the Aramaic term translated "Persians." It was likely a wordplay hinting that the division of the kingdom would be accomplished by the Persian army camped outside the city walls.

Prophecies of Babylon's Fall

This chapter records the fulfillment of prophecies predicting the downfall of Babylon (see Isa. 21:1–10; Jer. 51:39, 57). God is faithful and His Word is trustworthy. "Babylon has fallen, has fallen!" (Isa. 21:9).

■ *Because of Belshazzar's wickedness, God*
■ *had decreed an end to his reign. The king's*
■ *days were numbered and his kingdom*
■ *divided because his life did not measure up to*
■ *God's standard of righteousness.*

7. Daniel's Exaltation and the Fall of Babylon (5:29–31)

Daniel interpreted the writing and was given the rewards promised by the king. He did not refuse the gifts since to receive them now could not influence his message, and at any rate the gifts were meaningless. What good was it to be the third ruler of a defunct empire? That very night the city fell to the Medes and Persians and with it the last remnants of Babylonian dominance. Belshazzar was executed only a few hours later. Darius the Mede, who was "sixty-two" years of age, became ruler of Babylon.

Further Light on the Character of Belshazzar

Extrabiblical sources appear to corroborate Belshazzar's evil character. Ancient records seem to indicate that he was involved in the assassination of the previous Babylonian king (likely out of greed) and killed another man in a fit of jealousy.

■ *Those who foolishly challenge the Lord's*
■ *power will find they are no match for the liv-*
■ *ing God. Human beings may bring God's*
■ *temporal judgment on themselves through*
■ *gross sin.*

QUESTIONS TO GUIDE YOUR STUDY

1. What sins did Belshazzar commit? Which sin brought God's temporal judgment on him?

2. What was the message written on the wall in Belshazzar's banquet hall? What was the significance of the message?

3. What additional light do other ancient sources shed on the fall of Babylon?

DANIEL 6

VI. DANIEL IN THE LIONS' DEN (6:1–28)

"Daniel in the lions' den" is one of the most familiar stories in the Bible and, for that matter, in all of literature. The events recorded here took place soon after Babylon had fallen to the Persians, likely within the first or second year (539–537 B.C.). By this time the first group of Jewish captives under the leadership of Zerubbabel probably had returned to Palestine, and Daniel was over eighty years of age.

1. The New Government (6:1–3)

Darius wasted no time in organizing a government for the newly acquired empire, and he appointed 120 satraps (officials) to rule his kingdom. Over these satraps were three "administrators" ("commissioners," NASB; "presidents," NRSV, KJV), one of whom (better than "first", KJV's) was Daniel. The administrators watched over the satraps so that all tax moneys were properly collected and so that none of these lesser officials could steal from the king. Darius was impressed with Daniel and planned to set him over all the other officials in the kingdom.

■ *Daniel was rewarded for his faithful service*
■ *by being raised to a place of prominence in*
■ *the new Medo-Persian regime.*

Identity of Darius the Mede

The identification of Darius the Mede (5:31; chap. 6) is uncertain, but scholars have offered a number of suggestions. The two most likely possibilities are that Darius was a governor of Babylon (Gubaru, also called Gobryas, mentioned in a number of ancient texts) or was an alternative title for Cyrus. Dual titles were not uncommon. Since he was king of both Media and Persia, it might be expected that Cyrus the Persian (whose mother was a Mede) would have had another title such as Darius the Mede that pertained particularly to that portion of the empire. Daniel may also have followed a common Jewish practice (see Ezra 10:3; Talmud; Midrash) that reckoned a child of a mixed marriage according to maternal (in this case, Median) descent. Additionally, Darius the Mede was sixty-two years of age (5:31), the approximate age of Cyrus when Babylon fell in 539 B.C.

2. A Treacherous Plot (6:4–9)

Because the king planned to set Daniel over all the satraps and administrators, the jealousy of some of the other officials was aroused. They sought to discover some flaw in Daniel's character or professional ability in order to bring a charge against him to the king, but none was found. Certainly all 120 satraps were not party to this scheme, and the number was probably limited to a small handful. However, both of the other administrators were involved. These jealous officials concluded that there was only one area in which they might find a conflict between Daniel and the Persian government—in the area of his religion ("the law of his God").

A plot to topple Daniel from the king's good graces was hatched. The jealous officials encouraged Darius to issue a decree that no one should pray to any god or man except the king for thirty days. By this decree Darius would not be proclaiming himself to be a god, but during this thirty-day period he would act as mediator for the gods of all the nations subject to him. In his role as mediator, prayers to the gods were to be offered through the king rather than the priests.

Such a law might have been allowed for political reasons. It could have been used as a test of loyalty to Darius's new government, for in this manner subjects in Babylon would acknowledge the authority of Persia (and its deities). Those who broke the law were to be thrown into a den of lions where they would be torn to pieces and devoured.

Once signed, Darius's decree could not be changed.

- *Some of his fellow government officials*
- *planned to ensnare Daniel by forcing him to*
- *disobey the king in order to remain true to*
- *his faith. Daniel's choice would be to*
- *obey "the law of his God" or the law of*
- *human beings ("the laws of the Medes*
- *and Persians").*

3. The Accusation and Condemnation of Daniel (6:10–18)

(1) Daniel's Faithfulness (6:10)

Daniel was a man of courage and conviction. Even when he heard the law had been passed, he did not change his religious behavior. He went home, entered his upstairs room, opened the windows that faced toward Jerusalem, and prayed to the Lord his God. Daniel's custom was to pray three times a day, evidently at morning, afternoon, and night (see Ps. 55:17). The question here is not of a positive sin that Daniel would not commit but of a positive duty that he would not omit.

(2) The Accusation Against Daniel (6:11–15)

The officials began to spy on Daniel and soon observed what they had hoped for—Daniel praying to his God. They promptly reported Daniel's actions to the king.

When the king heard the charges against Daniel, "he was greatly distressed." However, Darius was not upset because Daniel had been praying (as the king's later actions demonstrate) but because for the first time he realized the real purpose of the law. It was not to honor him but to eliminate a rival of the jealous officials. The

Quality Service Rewarded

Daniel performed quality work in his position at the royal court. His dedication was rewarded by Nebuchadnezzar and Darius. Christians should be loyal and responsible employees, showing respect and giving their employers an honest day's work.

Not a Secret Disciple

Daniel's religious convictions were not hidden. The old prophet was not a secret disciple but a man who was not ashamed to let others know his allegiance was to the God of Israel. Believers today should be willing to express their faith in Christ openly (see Matt. 10:32–33; Rom. 1:16).

Jealousy

As in the story in chapter 3, jealous rivals attempted to put to death the innocent. Jealousy is a terrible sin.

The Lions' Den

The Assyrians and Persians captured lions and put them in cages, and so lions were available for the purpose of executing criminals. The word translated "den" may also mean "pit." This "den" may simply have been a large natural or man-made "pit" into which victims were thrown.

"The Laws of the Medes and Persians"

Daniel asserted that "the laws of the Medes and Persians" could not "be repealed" (cf. 6:8, 12, 15; Esther 1:19; 8:8). Secular sources confirm Daniel's testimony. The ancient writer, Diodorus of Sicily, reported the case of a man named Charidemus who was put to death under Darius III (ca. 336–330 B.C.). After being sentenced to death, the man was discovered to be perfectly innocent. Yet he was still executed because it was impossible to revoke what had been ordered by royal authority.

monarch understood that he had been duped by these evil men. That Daniel was well liked by Darius is clear from the story, and this added to the king's distress.

Darius had the law books searched to discover if there might be some legal loophole that could render the law unenforceable. Evidently, the law prescribed that the sentence be carried out the same day as the crime, and so Darius had only until sundown to solve the dilemma.

(3) The Sentence Carried Out (6:16–18)

After all attempts to save Daniel had failed, the king gave the order. Daniel was arrested and thrown into the den of lions. Darius's concern for his friend is touching. He shouted down to Daniel in the pit, "May your God, whom you serve continually, rescue you!" The fact that Darius believed it was possible for Daniel to be saved indicates that the prophet must have been telling the king of the great miracles the God of Israel had performed.

No one would dare remove the chain containing the names of the king and some of his highest officials. Daniel was now in the den, and all possibility of escape was cut off! When Darius returned to the palace, he refused all "entertainment" and began to fast for the prophet's safety.

■ *Daniel was willing to be faithful to his God*
■ *even though he knew it would probably cost*
■ *him his life.*

4. The Deliverance of Daniel (6:19–23)

At dawn the king rushed to the den to see if Daniel had survived the night. Babylonian custom was that the victim would be pardoned if he were tortured and had not died by the next day. The king's actions demonstrated that he held out the hope that Daniel's God could deliver him, but his "anguished" voice betrayed the fact that he did not believe it was likely. Great delight and astonishment must have over-whelmed Darius when he heard Daniel's voice. Daniel explained that God had sent His angel to protect him against the lions. Probably this was no ordinary angel, but God Himself. In many Old Testament passages, the angel of the Lord is equated with deity (see Gen. 16:11–14; Judg. 6:11–26).

When Daniel emerged from the pit, they found no mark of injury on him. The reason for Daniel's miraculous deliverance was stated: "He had trusted in his God."

■ *During Daniel's crisis, God was with him. By*
■ *grace the prophet was delivered because of*
■ *his faith in God.*

5. The Results (6:24–28)

(1) Accusers of Daniel Punished (6:24)

Daniel's integrity had been vindicated by the Lord Himself. Now the king commanded that those who had "falsely accused" the prophet should be thrown into the den of lions. Daniel had been guilty of breaking the law, but he had been falsely accused of disloyalty to the king. The number of persons executed was probably not large. Presumably only the other two administrators and a handful of the 120 satraps were involved in the scheme to kill Daniel.

Praying toward Jerusalem

The practice of praying toward Jerusalem was evidently based on the injunctions of Solomon in 1 Kings 8:35, 38, 44, 48 delivered at the dedication of the Temple (ca. 960 B.C.). Jerusalem was the place where Solomon's Temple had stood, and this edifice had symbolized the presence of Israel's God.

Posture in Prayer

Daniel knelt to pray (see 1 Kings 8:54; Ezra 9:5; Ps. 95:6), but at other times prayers were offered while standing (see Gen. 18:22ff.; 1 Sam. 1:26; Luke 18:13; Matt. 6:5). Praying with hands spread out toward heaven was also common (Ezra 9:5). Prayer itself is the key, not the posture of prayer.

The Question of Civil Disobedience

Daniel deliberately defied a law of the land. How may this action be reconciled with the scriptural admonition to obey civil authority (see Rom. 13:1–2)? Scripture does indeed instruct believers to obey the government, but the Bible also teaches that there is a higher law—the law of God. Peter and the other apostles told the Jewish authorities, "We must obey God rather than men!" (Acts 5:29).

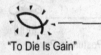

"To Die Is Gain"

The old prophet showed little concern for the consequences of his actions. He was over eighty years of age and may have felt the way Paul did when faced with death as an old man—willing to stay on earth if God willed it so but preferring to go to heaven to be with the Lord (Phil. 1:21–24).

(2) Daniel's God Honored (6:25–27)

The king was so impressed with this miracle that he issued a public decree ordering all people throughout the "land" to give proper recognition to the God of Daniel. Darius praised the Lord as "living," eternal, and powerful.

(3) Daniel Prospered (6:28)

"Prospered" apparently means that Daniel was elevated to the second highest position in the land under Darius, received great honor among the people, and was blessed in material ways. "During the reign of Darius and the reign of Cyrus the Persian" could also be translated, "during the reign of Darius, *even* (namely) the reign of Cyrus the Persian." If so, Daniel was specifying for the reader the identification of Darius the Mede—he was Cyrus the Persian.

■ *God's mighty acts bring glory to Himself and*
■ *are a witness to unbelievers.*

QUESTIONS TO GUIDE YOUR STUDY

1. Who might Darius the Mede have been?
2. What does the plot by the jealous officials reveal about Daniel's religious life?
3. Was Daniel justified in disobeying the king's order? Could you imagine a situation where believers today might be forced to disobey civil authority?
4. How is the virtue of faithfulness demonstrated in this chapter?

VII. DANIEL'S NIGHT VISION AND ITS MEANING (7:1–28)

Daniel 7 is the heart of the Book of Daniel and one of the most important passages in the Old Testament. The chapter is significant because it marks the literary turning point of the book from historical accounts to visions, had an enormous impact upon subsequent Jewish literature, and is of extreme significance prophetically. After 7:2, except for 10:1, the account is always in first person. Like the historical accounts in chapters 1–6, the visions of chapters 7–12 are recounted in chronological sequence.

1. Setting of the Vision (7:1)

In King Belshazzar's first year, Daniel received a vision from the Lord. Chronologically, Daniel's first vision occurred many years before the events of chapters 5 and 6.

Belshazzar's First Year

According to ancient Babylonian records, Nabonidus entrusted the kingdom to his son and left Babylon in his third year (553 B.C.). Daniel probably considered Belshazzar's first year to have begun at that time.

■ *Daniel and the Jewish people may have been*
■ *apprehensive concerning their future under*
■ *the rule of the wicked Belshazzar. For this*
■ *reason God may have chosen to reveal this*
■ *vision in the first year of the new king's reign*
■ *to reassure the Jews that He would protect*
■ *and sustain them.*

2. Details of the Vision (7:2–14)

(1) The Four Winds and the Great Sea (7:2)
Daniel saw four winds "churning up the great sea." A comparison of verse 3 and 17 indicates that the "sea" symbolizes the "earth," and the

beasts that rise out of this "sea" are interpreted later in the chapter to be great "earthly" kingdoms. Moreover, in the symbolism of Scripture the sea regularly stands for the peoples or nations of the earth (see Isa. 17:12–13; 57:20; cp. Rev. 13:1 with 13:11 and Rev. 17:1 with 17:15). Thus, the peoples of the earth are portrayed as a great sea of humanity in a constant state of unrest, chaos, and turmoil—an apt description of today's world.

The number "four" represents the four directions of the earth and signifies that the havoc created by the storm "winds" is universal. In this context, the winds seem to denote factors of all kinds that produce turmoil among the earth's nations throughout history. God's judgments are involved, but the turmoil described primarily results from the activities of persons who do not know God and the operation of Satan's forces on humanity.

(2) Beasts from the Sea (7:3)

In verse 17 the angel explained that the "four beasts" from the sea symbolized "four kingdoms" that would rise from the earth. They are the same empires represented by the statue's four metals in chapter 2—Babylon, Medo-Persia, Greece, and Rome. Both the animals themselves and the empires depicted by them were "different"—in size, power, and in many other ways.

(3) The Lion (7:4)

The first animal resembled an unusual looking lion (see Rev. 13:2) for it had large wings, like those of an eagle. Being named first, the lion rightly corresponded to the first part of the statue (the golden head), specifically stated to symbolize Babylon (see Dan. 2:38). The meaning of the symbolism in the last part of verse 4 is commonly understood as explained in the descriptions of Nebuchadnezzar presented in chapter 4. The lion's wings being torn off speaks of the king's insanity and loss of power, standing on two feet like a man and receiving a human heart (mind) denotes Nebuchadnezzar's humanitarian rule after his insanity, and the lion being "lifted up from the ground" indicates that it was God who raised the king to his place of honor.

(4) The Bear (7:5)

Medo-Persia followed Babylon as the next great world empire, and the "bear" was a fitting symbol of that kingdom noted for its great size and fierceness in battle. "Three ribs" in the bear's mouth represent the conquests of the empire, probably Medo-Persia's three major triumphs—Babylon (539 B.C.), Lydia (546 B.C.), and Egypt (525 B.C.). Persian dominion stretched from Egypt and the Aegean Sea on the west to the Indus River on the east.

(5) The Leopard (7:6)

Following Medo-Persia, Greece dominated the world. Two outstanding characteristics of a leopard—a beast of prey—are speed and an insatiable thirst for blood. "Four wings" on the leopard's back increased the speed of this already swift beast. Greece (under Alexander the Great) is aptly represented by this flying leopard for its conquests were carried out with lightning speed, and it had an insatiable lust for ever more territory. According to legend, Alexander wept because there were no more lands to conquer. In Scripture, "heads" may represent rulers or governments (see Dan. 2:38; Isa. 7:8–9; Rev. 13:3, 12), and that is the meaning here. Daniel predicted that this one empire (the leopard)

The Four Divisions of the Greek Empire

Alexander died in 323 B.C., and after much internal struggle the kingdom was carved into four parts by his generals. (1) Antipater, and later Cassander, gained control of Greece and Macedonia. (2) Lysimachus ruled Thrace and a large part of Asia Minor. (3) Seleucus I Nicator governed Syria, Babylon, and much of the Middle East (all of Asia except Asia Minor and Palestine). (4) Ptolemy I Soter controlled Egypt and Palestine.

would ultimately evolve into four kingdoms (four heads).

(6) The Unidentified Beast (7:7–8)

The fourth beast was the most "terrifying" and "frightening" because it was "very powerful" and "had large iron teeth" protruding from its mouth with which it "devoured" its prey. "Ten horns" with which to gore its victims were on its head, and Daniel pointed out later in the chapter that the beast had bronze claws (v. 19). This animal was "different" from the previous beasts because of its great power, fierce appearance, and because it was evidently larger in size. No name is given to the fourth beast because it did not look like any animal Daniel had ever seen. The fourth beast represented the Roman Empire that by the second century B.C. had superseded Greece as the dominant world power. Rome's might and cruelty are aptly depicted by Daniel's fourth beast.

"Horns" in Scripture commonly symbolize kings or kingdoms (see Rev. 13:1 and 17:12; also Ps. 132:17; Zech. 1:18), and the "ten horns" of verse 7 are specifically identified as "ten kings" in verse 24. Since the "horns" protruded from the fourth beast, these "kings" (or "kingdoms") must have a connection with ancient Rome.

Daniel saw "another horn, a little one" grow up among the ten. "Little" refers to the horn's size at the beginning (cp. v. 20). According to verse 24, the little horn symbolized a powerful king who would subjugate (uproot) three other kings (horns) by force.

He would be intelligent ("eyes," cp. Zech. 3:9; 4:10; Rev. 4:6; 5:6), arrogant, and would blaspheme the true God (see Dan. 7:25). The description of this evil, future king in these verses concurs with that found in other Scripture passages (see Dan. 11:36–37; 2 Thess. 2:3–12; Rev. 13:5–6). He is none other than the most infamous person in all of human history—the Antichrist.

A Comparison of The Beasts with the Statue of Chapter 2

BEASTS	STATUE	INTERPRETATION
Lion	Golden Head	Babylon
Bear	Silver Chest and Arms	Medo-Persia
Leopard	Bronze Belly and Thighs	Greece
Unidentified Beast	Iron Legs and Feet	Rome

(7) The Destruction of the Fourth Beast (7:9–12)

An awesome scene unfolded before Daniel's eyes. The "Ancient of Days" (the eternal God) took His seat on the throne and exercised His prerogative as the chief justice of the universe. White clothing depicted His absolute moral purity (see Isa. 1:18; Rev. 1:14). His white hair was a sign of old age and an apt symbol of God's eternal nature, already emphasized in this passage by the title "Ancient of Days." *Fire* is often representative of judgment, and God's throne on "wheels" (see Ezek. 1:15–21; 10:9–11) being engulfed in flames signified the great wrath ("a river of fire") of the Ancient of Days being poured out on the wicked. An

"The Books"

In Scripture "the books" (v. 10) are symbolic of the records kept in heaven of the deeds, words, and thoughts of every person who has ever lived (cf. Exod. 32:32; Dan. 12:1; Luke 10:20; Rev. 20:12).

innumerable angelic host (see Rev. 5:11) stood in God's presence.

According to verse 11, the evil empire will be totally annihilated and its leader judged (see Rev. 19:20). Verse 12 means that the other beasts, the first three empires, continued to live because they were absorbed into subsequent kingdoms.

(8) *The Kingdom of God (7:13–14)*

Surrounded by the clouds of heaven, "one like a son of man" (human appearance) made his grand entrance into the presence of the saints and angels. He was presented to the Ancient of Days (the custom in royal courts) and was given an eternal kingdom. Some scholars have identified this "son of man" as an angel or a personification of the people of God, the Jewish nation. The traditional view is that He is the Messiah, and the New Testament confirms this interpretation (see Matt. 24:30; Mark 14:61–62; John 12:34). Daniel 7:13 is the verse from Daniel that the New Testament quotes most frequently.

An Old Testament Glimpse of the Trinity

Two persons are distinguished in verses 13–14, the "son of man" and the "Ancient of Days." If the "son of man" is Christ (Messiah), the "Ancient of Days" who is also divine must be God the Father. Here then is an Old Testament glimpse of the plurality of persons in the Godhead. The Son was presented to the Ancient of Days that He might receive His Father's gift; namely, a universal kingdom (cf. Ps. 2:6–9).

- *Earthly kingdoms will rise and fall, but*
- *someday the kingdom of God will come and*
- *put an end to all wicked world rulers.*
- *Messiah will reign over this kingdom.*

3. *The Interpretation of the Vision (7:15–27)*

(1) *Identification of the Four Beasts (7:15–18)*

An angel explained to Daniel that the four beasts from the sea were four empires that would rise from the earth. When the four empires have run their course, the kingdom of God will come.

(2) Details of the Fourth Beast (7:19–26)

The fourth empire (beast) would dominate the world and crush all resistance to its rule (v. 23). Its ten horns representing, "ten kings," would emanate from the fourth kingdom—Rome (v. 24). "Another king" (little horn) would appear after the first ten and will be different from them. The little horn (vv. 8, 11, 20–22) has previously been identified as a person and is now interpreted as a king (ruler) of the last days. He is called in Scripture, among other names, the "man of lawlessness" (2 Thess. 2:3), the "Antichrist" (1 John 2:18), and the "beast" (Rev. 13:1ff.).

The little horn will be "different" from the other kings in that he will be greater in power ("will subdue three kings"), intelligence (symbolized by the eyes), and arrogance (mouth speaking boastful things). In the last days, he will rule the confederation of ten nations (kings). Evidently three of the ten kings will resist his power and be conquered by force; the others will then submit. This evil ruler will also blaspheme God (v. 25; see Rev. 13:5–6) and "oppress" the saints (see v. 21; Rev. 13:7).

Antichrist will attempt to abolish religious holidays ("set times") and religion altogether ("the laws"). Denying religious liberty is characteristic of dictators (e.g., Antiochus IV, Nero, Domitian, Stalin, Hitler). He will persecute the saints "for a time, times and half a time" (v. 25). Most scholars interpret this phrase to mean three and one-half years, though some understand it to signify an indefinite period.

Antichrist's doom and the destruction of his empire are set forth in verse 26. This will occur when the "son of man" (Dan. 7:13) returns

A Confederacy of Ten Horns

In the Book of Revelation (particularly chaps. 13 and 17), the apostle John also described a ten-horned confederacy led by a beast. Both kingdoms are opposed to God, and the leader of each blasphemes His name (see Dan. 7:25; Rev. 13:1, 5, 6).

"Oppress"

"Oppress" is a translation of an Aramaic word that literally means "to wear away" or "to wear out," as one would wear out a garment. Believers will daily be harassed until their lives become miserable. Religious freedom will be abolished (Dan. 9:27), and economic pressure will be applied to force citizens to follow this ruler and reject religion (see Rev. 13:16–17).

"A Time, Times and Half a Time"

In Dan. 12:7 this same phrase occurs and is taken to approximate the 1,290 days of 12:11 and 1,335 days of 12:12, both of which are just over three and one-half years. The phrase also appears in Rev. 12:14; and the duration of this period is explained in 12:6 to be 1,260 days—three and one-half years (cf. Dan. 4:16; 9:27; Rev. 11:2; 13:5).

from heaven with His holy angels and establishes His kingdom.

(3) The Kingdom of God (7:27)

When the fourth empire in its latter phase is destroyed, the everlasting kingdom of God will arrive. There will be universal peace and prosperity. The "saints" will reign with the King of the kingdom ("son of man") who will be worshiped by all.

■ *Earthly kingdoms dominate this present age,*
■ *but someday the kingdom of God will come.*
■ *Christ will then be universally honored and*
■ *worshiped.*

4. The Effect of the Vision on Daniel (7:28)

Daniel was "troubled" because he had seen many frightening things—kingdoms rising and falling, a diabolical tyrant, and the persecution of the saints. Moreover, he did not know when these things would occur.

Repetition of the Message

The vision of chapter 7 parallels the dream image of chapter 2. The revelation of the four kingdoms in Daniel likely was presented in two forms to underscore the certainty of this amazing prophecy.

■ *Uncertainty concerning the future may be*
■ *troubling, but we can trust in God.*

QUESTIONS TO GUIDE YOUR STUDY

1. When did Daniel receive his first vision? Why might God have given this vision to Daniel at this particular time?

2. What do the four beasts rising out of the sea symbolize?

3. Who is the "son of man"? Describe His kingdom.

4. Who is the "little horn"? Describe his character, actions, and judgment.
5. Why was Daniel troubled by what he had seen in the vision? Should the study of prophecy frighten us?

DANIEL 8

VIII. VISION OF THE RAM, THE GOAT, AND THE LITTLE HORN (8:1–27)

Daniel in this chapter reported his second vision, and once more animals were used to symbolize empires. In the previous chapter, God had given a preview of world history with emphasis on the end-times. God's people also needed to be warned of another crisis that would happen in less than four hundred years after Daniel's lifetime—the persecutions of a madman named Antiochus IV Epiphanes (175–163 B.C.). It would be one of the most horrible periods in history for Jewish believers, a time when the very existence of the true religion was threatened. God knew that for those brief—only a few years—but extremely dark days His people would need a supernatural revelation to encourage them as they faced their "great tribulation."

1. The General Setting (8:1–2)

Daniel's second vision came in the third year of Belshazzar's reign (ca. 550 B.C.) About this time Cyrus established the Medo-Persian Empire, destined to bring an end to the period of Babylonian supremacy within a mere twelve years. The whole world was anxiously watching to see what Cyrus would do. Possibly, God gave the vision at this time to assure Daniel that the Jews

"Susa"

Susa, ("Shushan," KJV) means "lily" was a city located about 220 miles east of Babylon and 150 miles north of the Persian Gulf (in modern Iran). At the time of Daniel's vision, it was the capital of Elam and later became one of the Medo-Persian royal cities. Darius I built a beautiful palace there. In 1901 archaeologists discovered the famous Code of Hammurabi in Susa. Both Esther and Nehemiah lived in this city (see Esther 1:2; Neh. 1:1).

Persia's Dominance

Before Cyrus came to power, Media was already a major force, but Persia was a small country holding less than fifty thousand square miles of territory. Cyrus succeeded in gaining control of powerful Media to the north (ca. 550 B.C.) and then made Persia the more important of the two states.

would survive as a people long after Cyrus (and Belshazzar) had passed from the scene.

Daniel may have been physically present in the fortress city ("citadel") of Susa or may have merely seen himself there in vision, probably the latter (see Ezek. 8–11; 40–48). The Ulai was an artificial canal about nine hundred feet wide that flowed near Susa on the northeast. Today the canal is dry.

■ *Like the vision of chapter 7, God may have*
■ *revealed this vision to reassure the Jewish*
■ *people that in spite of unsettled world events*
■ *they would survive.*

2. Contents of the Vision (8:3–14)

(1) The Ram (8:3–4)

Daniel beheld "a ram" with two horns (one longer than the other) standing beside the canal. In verse 20 the angel Gabriel interpreted this ram as the Medo-Persian Empire. The two horns denoted its two divisions, Media and Persia. The horn that grew up later and became longer signified the Persian division of the empire that began with less strength, but subsequently became more powerful than Media.

Medo-Persia made most of its conquests toward the west, north, and south. To the west it subdued Babylonia, Syria, Asia Minor, and made raids upon Greece; to the north—Armenia, Scythia, and the Caspian Sea region; to the south—Egypt and Ethiopia.

(2) The Goat (8:5–8)

In verse 21, Gabriel identified the goat as a symbol of the Greek Empire and the "prominent" horn as its first king (Alexander the Great). Coming "from the west" pointed to the position of Greece in relation to Medo-Persia. "Crossing the whole earth" meant that Alexander conquered the world of his day, and the goat speeding across the globe "without touching the ground" portrayed the swiftness of Alexander's conquests.

The "four prominent horns" are the four divisions of the Greek Empire that developed at Alexander's death (see 7:6 for discussion).

(3) The Little Horn (8:9–14)

From one of the divisions of the Greek Empire would emerge a king ("horn") of unusual significance (v. 9). This "horn" symbolized the eighth ruler of the Seleucid Greek Empire, Antiochus IV Epiphanes (175–163 B.C.). Antiochus IV was particularly important because of his exploits against the inhabitants of Palestine, and for that reason received special attention in the Book of Daniel (see 11:21–35). He had an insignificant ("small") beginning but became very powerful. He made notable conquests in "the south" (Egypt), "the east" (Persia, Parthia, Armenia), and "the Beautiful Land" (Palestine). Palestine is called "Beautiful" (see Dan. 11:16, 41; Jer. 3:19) because of its spiritual significance.

Antiochus persecuted the Jewish saints ("stars," "host"; interpreted in v. 24; cp. 12:3), blasphemed their God ("Prince of the host"), stopped the "daily sacrifice," desecrated the Temple with an idolatrous altar to Zeus, and attempted to destroy the Hebrew Scriptures ("truth"). He executed thousands of Jews who resisted his unfair regulations. In December 167 B.C. Antiochus committed his crowning act of sacrilege against the Jewish religion by erecting

Alexander the Great

Alexander was one of the great military strategists of history. He was born in 356 B.C., the son of a great conqueror in his own right, Philip of Macedon. Philip had united Greece with Macedonia and was planning to attack Persia when he was murdered. Alexander, educated under the famed Aristotle, was only twenty in 336 B.C. when he succeeded his father as king. A year and a half later (334 B.C.), he launched his attacks and within ten short years (by the age of thirty-two) had conquered the entire Medo-Persian Empire, including Syria, Palestine, Egypt, and the eastern territories to the borders of India. He died of a fever at Babylon in 323 B.C.

an altar to Zeus in the Temple precincts and offering swine on it (see 1 Macc. 1:37, 39, 44–47, 54, 59; 2 Macc. 6:2–5).

One "holy one" asked another, "How long will it take for the vision to be fulfilled . . . ?" By this the angel meant, How long would Temple worship be abolished and the persecution of the saints described in Daniel's vision continue? The answer was that 2,300 evenings and mornings would pass before the Temple would be "reconsecrated," and with it the end of the persecution. The time in question could involve only a total of 1,150 days since the 1,150 evening and 1,150 morning sacrifices (two sacrifices each day) equal a total of 2,300. This method of calculation results in a period of a little more than three years (ca. 167–164 B.C.).

Probably the 2,300 evenings and mornings represent a total of 2,300 days since in Old Testament usage an evening and morning specified a day (see Gen. 1). In that case the period in view would span six years and almost four months (ca. 170–164 B.C.). The general period of persecution under Antiochus began about 170 B.C. and concluded when Judas Maccabeus cleansed and "reconsecrated" the Temple on December 14, 164 B.C. (cf. 1 Macc. 4:52).

Today the Jews celebrate the Feast of Hanukkah ("dedication") to commemorate this momentous event.

1, 2 Maccabees

The apocryphal books of 1, 2 Maccabees contain a record of the persecutions of the Jewish people under Antiochus IV (see 1 Macc. 1–6; 2 Macc. 4–9).

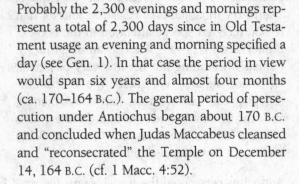

■ *God revealed that the Jewish people would go*
■ *through a time of suffering. This amazing*
■ *prophecy given centuries in advance of the*
■ *crisis would be a supernatural encourage-*
■ *ment to faithfulness. They were assured that*
■ *God would deliver them.*

3. The Interpretation of the Vision (8:15–26)
(1) The Interpreter (8:15–18)

The imposing figure who stood before Daniel (v. 15) may have been an angel, but probably this was a theophany, an appearance of God. Daniel does not seem to fear the angels (see Dan. 7:16), not even Gabriel (see 9:21ff.), but in verse 17 he exhibited extreme terror. Such fear is characteristic of those who have found themselves in the presence of the holy God (cf. Isa. 6:5; Ezek. 1:28; Rev. 1:17).

"From the Ulai" (v. 16) is literally "between the Ulai" River (that is, between its banks) and depicts this being as "hovering in the air" above the middle of the river (see Dan. 12:6–7).

The phrase, "the time of the end," must be understood in context. Sometimes it refers to the end of the age (11:40; 12:4), but here it seems to speak of the end of the events prophesied in this chapter—Antiochus's persecution of the Jews and their subsequent deliverance.

(2) The Interpretation (8:19–26)

"In the time of wrath" denotes the period when Antiochus and the unfaithful Israelites of the Maccabean period would be judged. Gabriel identified the "two-horned ram" as the Medo-Persian Empire (v. 20), the "shaggy goat" as the Greek Empire, and the goat's "large horn" as the first "king" of the empire, Alexander the Great (v. 21). Verse 22 meant that Alexander would die and the Greek Empire would be divided into four parts (see Dan. 8:8). None of these four kingdoms ever attained the power of Alexander's empire.

Verses 23–26 are the heart of the vision, and the reason for the revelation to Daniel. Antiochus IV would rise out of one division of the Greek

Gabriel

Verse 16 contains the first instance in Scripture where a good angel is designated by name. Gabriel is a prominent angel, also appearing to Zechariah, who was the father of John the Baptist (see Luke 1:19) and to Mary see (Luke 1:26). Michael (see 10:13, 21; 12:1; Jude 9; Rev. 12:7) is the only other good angel named in Scripture.

"Son of Man"

In 8:17 "son of man" is not the same in the original language as in 7:13 and has a different meaning. Here the expression emphasized Daniel's weakness and mortality, 'adam ("man") connoting that which is from the ground, earthly (a mere mortal). In Ezekiel the term is used approximately one hundred times in this sense.

Empire (Seleucid) and toward the end of its dominance. The "rebels" are best taken to be Jews who have forsaken their God. Antiochus would be harsh ("stern-faced"), adept at political "intrigue," powerful, cause "devastation," be successful, "destroy" many human lives, be deceitful, arrogant, a blasphemer ("stand against the Prince of princes"), and persecute the saints (vv. 23–25). "Not by his own power" (v. 24) probably alludes to Satan, who will inspire this evil king. He will be "destroyed" by God ("not by human power").

Gabriel reassured Daniel that the revelation was "true" and would be fulfilled (v. 26). Ancient documents were sealed for their preservation, and this is the idea here. Daniel was instructed to take measures to ensure that the vision's contents would be available for future generations (see Dan. 12:4). Antiochus IV lived almost four hundred years after Daniel ("the distant future").

Antiochus's Death

According to 1 Maccabees 6:1–16, Antiochus died (in 163 B.C.) of grief and remorse in Persia after being defeated in the siege of the city of Elymais and receiving word that his forces had been routed by the Jews in Palestine

See 2 Macc. 9:1–28; Josephus, *Antiquities* 12.9.1.

■ *A difficult time for the Jews was coming, but*
■ *God promised that He would deliver them.*

4. The Effect on Daniel (8:27)

Daniel was quite old, and he suffered a severe emotional and physical reaction to the vision. Afterward, the prophet rose from his sick bed and "went about the king's business." Daniel still did not grasp the full significance of all he had seen and heard. For example, when would these things happen and who was this evil king who would oppress his people?

Antiochus IV has been called the Old Testament "Antichrist" and may even be a type of the future

Antichrist. There are striking parallels between the lives of these two individuals. For example, both are symbolized by horns that were "little" or "small" at the beginning (7:8; 8:9), have great power (8:24; 11:39; 2 Thess. 2:9; Rev. 13:7–8), are energized by Satan (8:24; 2 Thess. 2:9; Rev. 13:2), persecute believers (8:24; 7:21, 25; Rev. 13:7), deceive (8:25; 2 Thess. 2:9; Rev. 13:4, 14; 19:20), are proud (8:25; 7:8, 11, 20, 25; 2 Thess. 2:4; Rev. 13:5), blaspheme God (8:25; 7:25; 11:36; 2 Thess. 2:4; Rev. 13:5–6), and are not killed by human hand (8:25; 2 Thess. 2:8; Rev. 19:19–20).

■ *Daniel understood much concerning the*
■ *vision, but there was much that was still*
■ *unclear. Our understanding of prophecy is*
■ *similar. We will not understand many details*
■ *of prophecy until the time is near.*

QUESTIONS TO GUIDE YOUR STUDY

1. What did the ram and the goat in Daniel's vision signify?
2. What evil king's life is described in this chapter?
3. Who was the first holy angel named in Scripture?
4. What was the significance of this vision for the Jewish people?

IX. VISION OF THE SEVENTY SEVENS (9:1–27)

Although the message revealed to Daniel in this chapter is called a "vision" (see v. 23), Daniel did not see animals rising out of a sea or rams and goats as in the previous two visions. Neither did Gabriel appear in vision but in bodily form. Therefore the "vision" of chap. 9 may be thought of more as a prophetic revelation (see Prov. 29:18; Obad. 1; Nah. 1:1; Hab. 2:2).

Daniel 9 contains a record of the prophet's prayer on behalf of the covenant people, Israel, and God's response to that prayer. Primarily for this reason, the covenant name, LORD (Jehovah or Yahweh), appears in this chapter (seven times), although it is not found elsewhere in the book.

1. Occasion of the Vision: Daniel's Prayer (9:1–19)

These verses record one of the truly great prayers in the Bible. It is an excellent pattern for believers today as they come before God's throne of grace.

(1) Circumstances of the Prayer (9:1–2)

Daniel received this revelation in the first year of Darius the Mede (ca. 538 B.C.), approximately twelve years after his second vision (chap. 8). The prophet would now have been over eighty years of age. If Darius was another name for Cyrus (see discussion at 6:1), Xerxes ("Ahasuerus," KJV, NRSV, NASB) was a title applied to his father.

As Daniel studied the Scriptures, he observed Jeremiah's prediction that Judah would return

"LORD"

Daniel addressed his petition "to the LORD." LORD is the translation of the Hebrew, "Yahweh" or "Jehovah," the particular name of Israel's God. The name, Yahweh, was associated early with the gracious, covenant-keeping God of Israel (see Exod. 6:2–8), and Daniel's use of the appellation would in itself be a reminder to God of His relationship to His people. Yahweh was about to be asked to keep the covenant promises that He had made to Israel.

from the Babylonian exile after seventy years (Jer. 25:11, 12; 29:10). The captivity period began with the first deportation in 605 B.C. and ended when the Jews returned not long after 539 B.C. Approximately seventy years had passed. This was an amazing prophecy. Three other noteworthy items may be observed in verse 2. Jeremiah's writings were "the word of the Lord," they were already considered to be Scripture, and Daniel believed in the reality of predictive prophecy.

(2) Manner of the Prayer (9:3)

Daniel prayed fervently to the Lord with a determined heart. "Fasting" demonstrated to God the prophet's deep concern, and being clothed in "sackcloth" (coarse, rough cloth) and sitting in "ashes" were expressions of humility that commonly accompanied fasting (cf. Esther 4:1–3).

(3) Contents of the Prayer (9:4–19)

Daniel's prayer contains many similarities to earlier Old Testament passages, particularly Deuteronomy, Solomon's prayer in 1 Kings 8, and Jeremiah. This prayer is a model for believers as they approach God. It began with adoration of the Lord (v. 4), was followed by confession of personal and national sin (vv. 5–14), and concluded with the prophet's petition (vv. 15–19). This is the proper order, for only after the Lord is praised and sin confessed is the believer qualified to offer requests to the holy God.

Daniel addressed the Lord as, "my God"—the basis on which he was able to approach the Lord with his requests.

ADORATION (9:4B)

Daniel praised the Lord as "great," "awesome," faithful, and loving. Love and obedience to

"Covenant of Love"

NIV's "covenant of love" is literally, "the covenant and the love," and the literal translation seems to convey more exactly the idea. Both terms are definite, singular nouns and therefore refer to a particular "covenant" and a particular kind of "love." Since the point of Daniel's prayer is that the Jews might return to their land and continue as a nation, the Abrahamic "covenant" must be in view, for it was in this covenant that God specifically promised to Abraham a land and national existence for his descendants, Israel (see Gen. 12:1–3; 15:18–21). The "love" is that loyal love of God by which He faithfully keeps His promises to His people, in this case, those of the covenant. Today all those who have received Christ have entered into a covenant relationship with God and experience His love as His spiritual children.

"Sinned"

The Hebrew verb (*chata'*) translated "sinned" in verse 5 basically means "to miss the mark." For example, Judges 20:16 says that there were seven hundred Benjamite soldiers who "could sling a stone at a hair and not *miss* (*chata'*)" the target. Ethically speaking, sin is missing God's mark or goal of holy living that is required of all human beings (Rom. 3:23). Israel as a nation fell short of God's design to be a holy people.

"The Curses and Sworn Judgments" (v. 11)

In Deuteronomy 28:15ff., the contents of this curse are recorded. It included poor crops, infertility, disease, lack of rain, defeat before enemies, and the most terrible penalty of all, expulsion from the land of Canaan.

God demonstrate that one has entered into God's family.

CONFESSION (9:5–14)

Daniel set forth six different aspects of Israel's sin in verses 5–6. Israel had "sinned," "done wrong," "been wicked," "rebelled," "turned away" from Yahweh's commands and laws, and "not listened" to Yahweh's prophets. What an indictment!

In verse 7 the righteousness of the Lord is contrasted with the unfaithfulness of Israel. Israel was humiliated by being defeated by an enemy and taken captive from her land (vv. 7–8). In spite of the nation's rebellion, God is "merciful" and "forgiving," (v. 9). Because Israel had forsaken God's law, the judgments promised in the Law of Moses had "been poured out on" the nation (vv. 11–12).

Daniel declared that Israel's judgment was unique. Certainly other nations had experienced defeat and deportation, but their gods were in reality not gods (see Ps. 135:15–17; Isa. 44:9ff.). Yet Israel's God was unlike the gods of the nations. He was the real God, and the Jews were His people. How could such a catastrophe fall on the people of the God of the universe?

In spite of this calamity, the nation as a whole still had not repented (v. 13). God brought the "disaster" of the exile on Judah because He is "righteous" and judges sin (v. 14).

PETITION (9:15–19)

In verse 15 the prophet recalled God's awesome display of power during the Egyptian Exodus. God had delivered Israel from an impossible situation before, and the implied request was for Him to do it once more. Daniel petitioned God to restore both Jerusalem (v. 16) and the Temple (v. 17). "Look with favor" is literally "cause your face to shine" (see Num. 6:25). Daniel prayed for the Temple to be restored "for your sake, O Lord" (see v. 19). Not only was the destroyed Temple a disgrace for God's people but for the Lord Himself. The nations would think that Israel's God was weak and insignificant if He was unable to protect His own sanctuary. Daniel's prayer reached a passionate crescendo in verses 18–19 as the prophet pleaded for God to intervene on their behalf—"give ear," "hear," "open your eyes," "see," "listen," "forgive," "hear," "act," and "do not delay."

■ Daniel praised the Lord, confessed sin, and
■ pleaded fervently that God would restore his
■ nation. His requests were based on God's
■ great mercy.

2. Mediator of the Vision (9:20–23)

While Daniel was still praying (v. 20), suddenly the angel Gabriel appeared to him (v. 21).

Gabriel (see 8:15, 16) is called a "man" because he appeared in human form. Apparently Gabriel is the chief angel for divine communication (see Luke 1:19, 26–27). "In swift flight" could also be rendered, "in my extreme weariness," or something similar (cf. NASB). If the idea of "weariness" is adopted, it must apply to Daniel for weariness as affecting an angel is absurd.

Do All Angels Have Wings?

Some angels (i.e., cherubs and seraphs) are portrayed in Scripture as having wings and flying (cf. Exod. 25:20; Isa. 6:2; Ezek. 1:6, 11, 19, 24),

"As It Is Written"

In verse 13 we find the first instance of the expression that became so common in the New Testament and in Rabbinic literature—"as it is written."

Intercessory Prayer

Daniel interceded for his nation. God has also given modern believers the responsibility and privilege of interceding for their nation (see 1 Tim. 2:1–2).

Sinless Perfection

Daniel confessed not only the sin of his people but his own sin (v. 20). He was one of the greatest saints who ever lived, and yet he still had not reached the point where he could say, "I have kept my heart pure; I am clean and without sin" (Prov. 20:9). Even after the believer has been saved, there will be need for confession of sin.

"Highly Esteemed"

Daniel was "highly esteemed" (v. 23; "greatly beloved," NRSV, KJV). "Highly esteemed" is a translation of a Hebrew word that describes something or someone desired or counted precious. A plural form of the word is employed in the Hebrew language to indicate great value. The term is used to speak of the value of gold (Ezra 8:27) and costly garments (Gen. 27:15). Thus, Daniel was considered to be a "very precious treasure" to the Lord, as are all of His children.

but angels usually appear in human form. Gabriel appeared in the form of a "man," and men do not have wings.

The time of the "evening sacrifice" was between about 3:00 P.M. and 4:00 P.M. No literal sacrifice was made in Babylon, but this was a time of day commonly used for prayer (see Ezra 9:5; Ps. 141:2). "As soon as" Daniel had begun to pray, the Lord sent Gabriel with an answer (v. 23).

■ *Sincere prayer touches the heart of God. The*
■ *angel Gabriel was sent from heaven with an*
■ *answer to Daniel's prayer.*

3. Substance of the Vision (9:24–27)

What follows is one of the most astounding prophecies in the Bible.

(1) Period of Time (9:24a)

"Sevens" (traditionally "weeks") is a literal translation of the Hebrew term and refers to periods of seven without specifying what the units are. The two most common views are that they are indefinite periods of time or sevens of years.

OLD TESTAMENT "SEVENS"

Daniel's Jewish audience was familiar with the concept of "sevens" of years because the sabbatical year observance was based on this premise (see Lev. 25:1–7; 26:33–35; 2 Chron. 36:21). For this reason sevens of years was probably Daniel's meaning. If so, "seventy sevens" equaled 490 years.

(2) People (9:24b)

"Your people" has been interpreted to refer to the church. However, since Daniel's people were the Jews and his "holy city" was Jerusalem, the prophecy would seem to refer to the nation of Israel and the city of Jerusalem.

(3) Accomplishments (9:24c)

God's purpose for the "seventy sevens" is to accomplish some wonderful goals. Sin will cease and a period of eternal "righteousness" will come. Atonement for wickedness would be made by Christ on the cross. All prophecy will be fulfilled. "To anoint the most holy" may denote either the anointing of a holy person or a holy place. Some have understood Christ's anointing for ministry to be intended here. Yet all thirty-nine instances of the phrase, "the most holy" (lit., "holy of holies"), in the Old Testament refer to the tabernacle or Temple. This "most holy" place probably is the future Temple described by Daniel's contemporary, Ezekiel (see Ezek. 40–48). This Temple will be built and consecrated for service when Christ returns.

(4) Beginning of the Seventy Sevens (9:25a)

The seventy sevens would commence with a "decree" to "rebuild Jerusalem" (destroyed by the Babylonians in 586 B.C.). Cyrus's proclamation issued in 538 B.C. (Ezra 1:2–4; 6:3–5) and decrees by Artaxerxes I in 458 B.C. (Ezra 7:11–26) and 445 B.C. (Neh. 2:5–8) have been suggested. The decree to Ezra in 458 B.C. seems to fulfill the requirements of the prophecy better than the others.

(5) Events of the First Sixty-nine Sevens (9:25b–26)

During this period, a number of significant events would transpire. Jerusalem would be restored, but most importantly, an Anointed One would come who would be "cut off." Some

"Cut Off"

"Cut off" (v. 26) frequently denotes the cutting off by death in the Old Testament (Exod. 12:15, 19; Lev. 7:20; Num. 9:13; Ps. 37:28, 38; Isa. 53:8). Here it refers to Christ's atoning death on the cross.

time after this last occurrence, Jerusalem and the Temple would again be destroyed during a time of war.

"In times of trouble" refers to the struggles involved in rebuilding Jerusalem during Nehemiah's governorship (see Neh. 4:1ff.; 9:36–37). Sixty-nine sevens (483 years) would pass from the decree to rebuild Jerusalem until the "Anointed One" came (v. 25) and be "cut off" (v. 26). The statement that "the Anointed One" would be "cut off" and the teaching concerning Messiah's person and work elsewhere in Scripture confirm that this individual is Jesus Christ.

If Artaxerxes's first decree began the sevens, 483 years after 458 B.C. would result in a date of A.D. 26, the time of Jesus' baptism. Jesus' anointing for ministry came at His baptism (see Matt. 3:16); thus, He became the "Anointed One" at that time, an amazing prophecy.

"And will have nothing" means that when Christ died, His earthly ministry seemed to have been in vain. His disciples had deserted Him, and from all appearances He had not accomplished what He had set out to do. After the resurrection, however, all of this changed.

Gabriel had already revealed to Daniel that Jerusalem would be rebuilt after the Babylonian destruction, but now he informed the prophet that sometime in the future Jerusalem and the Temple would again be destroyed by "the people of the ruler who will come." Historically, the next destruction of Jerusalem and the Temple after the Babylonian period was that perpetrated by the Romans in A.D. 70.

(6) Events of the Seventieth Seven (9:27)

Some scholars interpret verse 27 to speak of Christ's work in the first century. He would confirm a salvation "covenant" and make "sacrifice and offering" unnecessary by His death on the cross. Others believe that this verse refers to the activities of Antichrist ("the ruler who will come," v. 26). The verse would mean that the Antichrist will make a "covenant" ("a treaty," see Gen. 14:13; 21:27, 32; 31:44; Obad. 7) with the Jewish people for the last "seven" (seven years). In the middle of this seven-year period, he will stop all religious activities (see 7:25). His atrocities ("abomination") will continue until God's "decreed" judgment is "poured out on him" at the end of the age (see Dan. 7:9–11, 26; 2 Thess. 2:8; Rev. 19:19–21).

■ *Daniel was assured that his beloved Jerusa-*
■ *lem and its Temple would be rebuilt. Greater*
■ *still, the promised Messiah would appear,*
■ *although He would die. Eventually the king-*
■ *dom of God would come, and all the prom-*
■ *ised blessings of verse 24 (made possible by*
■ *Messiah's death) would be fulfilled. This*
■ *prophecy should be of great comfort to*
■ *believers today.*

QUESTIONS TO GUIDE YOUR STUDY

1. What may we learn about the Scriptures from Dan. 9:2?

2. What elements do we find in Daniel's prayer?

3. What great goals of history will be accomplished by the events of the seventy sevens?

4. What specific prophetic events are set forth in 9:24–27? How does a study of these verses benefit modern believers?

DANIEL 10

X. DANIEL'S FINAL VISION (10:1–12:13)

Daniel's last recorded vision extends from 10:1 through 12:13. In this vision an angel appeared to the prophet and revealed to him the history of Israel from the Persian period (the time when the vision was given) until the coming of the kingdom of God.

1. The Preparation for the Vision (10:1–11:1)

(1) Setting (10:1–3)

Daniel's final "revelation" came "in the third year of Cyrus king of Persia" (v. 1). The four visions (chaps. 7–12) appeared in two groups of two: the first and third years of Belshazzar and the first and third years of Cyrus. Cyrus's third year would have been 536/535 B.C., two years after Gabriel's appearance to Daniel in chapter 9 and a short while after the first return of the Jewish exiles to Palestine. About this time the lions' den incident took place, although it is not certain if it happened shortly before or after the vision.

Verse 1 forms a general statement of introduction to the vision, and the third person seems to have been chosen for that reason. Daniel interjected his Babylonian name, "Belteshazzar," apparently to emphasize that he was indeed the same individual spoken of earlier in the book.

The vision "concerned a great war." "War" is a translation of a Hebrew word that means "army, war, warfare, or service." Probably all the conflicts (or warfare) recorded in these last chapters are involved in the expression, whether conflicts between nations or angels.

Evidently, the prophet was again praying for wisdom concerning the future of his people, the Jews. By now the Jewish captives had returned to Palestine, but their plight was precarious. Work on the Temple was being opposed by the Samaritans, and it is possible that reconstruction had already been halted (see Ezra 4:5, 24). This development may have led to the prophet's renewed concern. Daniel's mourning over the plight of his people involved prayer (v. 12) and fasting (v. 3; see also Matt. 9:14–15).

"Three weeks" (v. 3) is literally "three sevens of days," days being added to distinguish between the "sevens" of chapter 9. Daniel seemed to have engaged in a type of fast ("no choice food; no meat or wine") rather than refraining from eating all food during this period. Apparently, he existed on bread and water. "Lotions" were commonly used by the Jews and other ancient peoples to soothe and refresh the skin and to protect against the heat.

Fasting is a neglected discipline for most Christians today, but it was a biblical practice. Some have associated fasting with legalism, but only one fast was commanded in the biblical law code—the Day of Atonement (see Lev. 16:29–31).

(2) Vision of the Heavenly Being (10:4–9)

Passover was celebrated in "the first month" (on the fourteenth day), and possibly the season of the year had been a factor in Daniel's decision to fast and pray. Since Passover was the time of Israel's deliverance from Egypt, Daniel's

"Mourned"

"Mourned" (v. 2) is a participle in the Hebrew language which has the force of "continually mourning," a state of mourning. The Hebrew word translated "mourned," denotes mourning for the dead (Gen. 37:34), over sin (Ezra 10:6), and over a calamity (Ezek. 7:12). Years later Nehemiah (Neh. 1:4) "mourned" over the condition of the Jews who had returned to Palestine, and this is evidently what so deeply concerned Daniel.

The Question of Fasting Today

Fasting is a personal matter between the individual and God. It is voluntary. Nevertheless, if giants of the faith like Moses, David, Esther, Daniel, Paul, and Jesus Himself felt the need to fast, it would seem reasonable that modern saints should be willing to deny themselves in order to pray more earnestly for the furtherance of the kingdom of God in a world that lies in deep spiritual darkness.

Tigris River

The Tigris River originated several hundred miles to the north of Babylon and flowed through Babylonia to the Persian Gulf, passing within about twenty miles of the capital. Consequently, Daniel may have been as close as twenty miles or as far as several hundred miles from the city of Babylon. Due to his great age, he probably did not travel great distances and was not far from the city.

thoughts may have turned toward the present deliverance and "exodus" of the Israelites from Babylon. Daniel probably had left the capital in order to spend uninterrupted time with the Lord. While the prophet "was standing on the bank" of the Tigris River, an awe-inspiring heavenly being appeared.

This heavenly being, called a "man" because he appeared in human form, was dressed in white "linen" garments. Priests (see Exod. 28:42; Lev. 6:10; 16:4) and the angel in Ezek. 9:2, 3, 11; 10:2, 6, 7 (see Rev. 15:6) are specifically stated to have been arrayed in white "linen." Here the significance of the "linen" is its white color, white being symbolic of purity (see Isa. 1:18; Dan. 11:35; 12:10). Saints in heaven are also depicted as wearing white robes (see Rev. 3:5; 6:11; 7:9, 13), and earlier in this book God Himself was described as being clothed in white garments (7:9). The golden belt was worn by the wealthy and royal classes in the ancient Near East. In this context, the symbolism may suggest a king or judge.

His body looked like "chrysolite" ("beryl," KJV, NASB, NRSV), some kind of gold-colored precious stone (see Ezek. 1:16; 10:9). His face appeared as brilliant as a flash of "lightning," and his eyes were like "flaming torches." "His arms" and "legs" gleamed like "burnished bronze," indicating that his body had a fiery appearance, like burning metal (see Ezek. 1:27). "His voice" thundered like "the sound of a multitude" of people speaking.

Many Bible scholars have identified the "man dressed in linen" as the angel sent to deliver the message to Daniel (10:10ff.). Others have held that He was God, namely Jesus Christ. That this person is divine seems to be correct, not only because of the overwhelming effect His presence had on Daniel, but because of the similar description of the theophany (divine appearance) presented in Ezek. 1:26–28 and the even closer parallel in the portrait of Christ in Rev. 1:12–16. In Daniel 12:6 this "man in linen" also seemed to have knowledge that transcended that of the other angels, and in 12:7 He took a divine oath.

An argument raised against the equation of this person with deity is that the angel described in 10:10ff. is clearly inferior to God (see 10:11, 13). The proper solution to the problem is that the "man dressed in linen" and the interpreting angel introduced in verse 10 are distinct personalities. In the Book of Revelation there is a similar pattern. On occasions John encountered Christ Himself (Rev. 1:12–20), whereas at other times he was instructed by an angel (see Rev. 17:1–6).

Only Daniel witnessed the theophany, even though the men with him felt a supernatural presence and "fled" in "terror" (v. 7). Paul had a similar experience when he met Christ on the Damascus road (Acts 9:1–7). Daniel was overwhelmed with shock and fell unconscious (v. 9; see Rev. 1:17).

(3) The Interpreting Angel's Explanation (10:10–14)

Unlike the two previous visions (see Dan. 8:16; 9:21), the interpreting angel was not named, but many scholars identify him as Gabriel. As in 9:23, Daniel was addressed as one "highly esteemed" (v. 11). Daniel was heard when he first began to pray, but for twenty-one days "the prince of the Persian kingdom" had prevented

Christ's Glory

The symbolism in Dan. 10:5–6 describes Jesus Christ as holy (white linen), important (golden belt), judge (fiery appearance), glorious (face like lightning), omniscient (eyes like fire), and authoritative (voice like a multitude). Since Christ is the glorious, almighty God, all persons should submit to Him as Lord and Savior.

"Michael"

Michael (whose name means "who is like God?") is introduced in verse 13 and is also mentioned in Dan. 10:21; 12:1; Jude 9; and Rev. 12:7 in Scripture. In Jude 9, he is called the "archangel" which means "first (chief) angel." Michael was assigned by God as Israel's prince (see Dan. 10:21); he was "great" in power and protected the Jewish people (cp. 12:1). Since Israel has a mighty angelic supporter in the heavenly realm, its existence was assured for no earthly power can resist this great prince.

Gabriel from bringing the answer to the prophet (vv. 12–13). Michael apparently became involved because Daniel was interceding for Israel, and Michael is specifically stated to be Israel's "prince" (see v. 21). With Michael's help, Gabriel had victory over his foe and was able to continue his journey.

Who was this "prince of the Persian kingdom" who resisted Gabriel for three weeks? First, he must have been an angel since no human prince could have withstood Gabriel. Moreover, Israel's "prince" was the angel Michael (10:21), and it is reasonable to suppose that in the same context the "prince" of Persia was also an angel. Second, inasmuch as this prince opposed God's angel, he may safely be assumed to be an evil angel—a demon. Third, he is called the "prince of the Persian kingdom," so Persia must have been his special area of activity. Persia ruled the world of the day, and Satan would have concentrated his efforts in this most influential area. The angelic warfare continued, for verse 20 reveals that the good angel would return to fight against this demon.

Daniel's experience should not be interpreted to signify that God is weak or that demonic forces have power to thwart the will of God. The Book of Daniel teaches throughout its pages the absolute sovereignty of the Almighty, and God could easily have ensured the delivery of the message to Daniel in an instant. Within the omniscient wisdom of God and the divine plan of God, this delay was permitted.

Daniel's prayer had been for insight concerning the future of his people, the Jews, and God granted him knowledge concerning these matters (v. 14).

"In the Future"

"In the future" (v. 14) is a translation of a Hebrew phrase usually rendered, "in the latter days." It normally describes events that will occur just prior to and including the coming of the kingdom of God.

(4) Daniel Strengthened to Understand the Vision (10:15–11:1)

Daniel was "speechless" with fright, but Gabriel strengthened him (vv. 15–18). The prophet was again designated as one "highly esteemed" (cp. 9:23; 10:11) by the Lord (v. 19).

Parenthetically, the angel announced that soon he must "return to fight against the prince of Persia," a battle that would continue for the two centuries of Persian rule (539–331 B.C.). This struggle involved all of the decisions and relationships pertaining to the Jews during the Persian period (e.g., the reconstruction of the Temple, deliverance for the Jews during the time of Esther, permission for Ezra and Nehemiah to return to Jerusalem, and their subsequent construction of the city).

The angel added that later "the prince of Greece will come," implying that he would fight against this prince as well. In keeping with the identification of the previously mentioned prince of Persia, "the prince of Greece" would be a demonic angel. Angelic support for God's people would be needed then, for chapter 11 details many of the struggles of the Jews during the Greek period, especially the crisis during the rule of Antiochus IV. The "Book of Truth" (v. 21) figuratively refers to God's plan for Israel and the world, not merely the revelation entrusted to Daniel.

Gabriel added that there was no one to help him in his fight against the princes of Persia and Greece "except Michael, your prince." No one except Michael supported Gabriel in his spiritual warfare—not because no one else was available but because no one else was needed.

Delayed Answers to Prayers

God's reasons for delaying answers to prayers are not always clear. Many times God permits believers to wait for their prayer answers in order to teach them valuable lessons (e.g., spiritual commitment, patience, faith). There are also times when God fully intends to respond affirmatively to a request, but in His wisdom delays because He knows that the proper time has not yet come.

Angels

Daniel 10 communicates several important facts about angels. (1) Angels are real. (2) There are good and evil angels. (3) Angels may influence the affairs of human beings. (4) There is an invisible, spiritual warfare being waged that involves angels and believers (cf. Eph. 6:12). (5) God's angels act on behalf of the saints. Believers probably would be surprised to learn of the many acts performed for them (e.g., protection) by the Lord's angels.

In 11:1 Gabriel related that he had helped Michael in some manner "in the first year of Darius the Mede" (ca. 538 B.C., two years before this vision). Since Michael (Israel's prince) was involved, the conflict must have concerned the Jewish people. The text does not name the occasion of this particular struggle, but it probably involved Cyrus's decree to allow the Jews to return to Palestine. Cyrus released the Jews, but unknown to the Persian monarch angelic forces played a part in that decision.

- *Daniel prayed and fasted for three weeks.*
- *God honored his prayer by sending an angel*
- *with an answer. Although it may take time,*
- *God always answers our prayers.*

QUESTIONS TO GUIDE YOUR STUDY

1. Is fasting a practice that Christians should observe today?
2. What are the two views concerning the person of 10:5–6?
3. Who was the "prince of the Persian kingdom"?
4. What may we learn about angels from Daniel 10?
5. How may we explain Gabriel's delay in reaching Daniel? How may this be understood in light of the omnipotence of God?

2. The Vision (11:2–12:3)

In the previous section the fourth vision was introduced; now its contents—a history of key events leading up to the end—are revealed. Emphasis is placed on the activities of two individuals, Antiochus and Antichrist. Historical details (revealed hundreds of years in advance) set forth in this prophecy are astounding.

(1) Prophecies Concerning Persia (11:2)

After Cyrus (see Dan. 10:1) three kings (Cambyses, Smerdis, and Darius I) governed Persia before a fourth particularly significant ruler came to power. Xerxes I (486–465 B.C.) is clearly identified as the fourth king by the description of his great wealth and expedition against Greece. Kings after Xerxes are not mentioned, apparently because the later Persian rulers were not germane to the writer's purpose. The most likely reason for this is that the counterattack of Alexander, referred to in the next verse, was particularly encouraged by the massive military campaign launched against Greece by Xerxes I.

(2) Prophecies Concerning Greece (11:3–4)

The "mighty king" is Alexander the Great (336–323 B.C.) who brought about the downfall of the Persian Empire. The description of his exploits and his kingdom are unmistakable. Moreover, Antiochus IV Epiphanes, a Seleucid-Greek ruler, proceeded out of one of the four divisions of this mighty king's realm see vv. 21ff.). When Alexander died, his generals partitioned the empire into four parts (see 7:6; 8:8). Alexander's sons (Alexander IV and Herakles) were murdered, and so no part of his territory went to "his descendants."

Ptolemaic and Seleucid Kings in Daniel 11:5–20

PTOLEMAIC	SELEUCID	REFERENCE
Ptolemy I Soter (323–285 B.C.)	Seleucus I Nicator (312/ 11–280 B.C.)	(11:5)
Ptolemy II Philadelphus (285–246 B.C.)	Antiochus II Theos (261–246 B.C.)	(11:6)
Ptolemy III Euergetes (246–221 B.C.)	Seleucus II Callinicus (246–226 B.C.)	(11:7–9)
Ptolemy IV Philopator (221–203 B.C.); Ptolemy V Epiphanes (203–181 B.C.)	Antiochus III (the Great; 223–187 B.C.)	(11:10–19)
	Seleucus IV Philopator (187–175 B.C.)	(11:20)

The Septuagint

According to tradition, Ptolemy II Philadelphus (11:6) instigated a translation of the Hebrew Bible into Greek called the Septuagint (abbreviated as LXX). This highly successful translation of the Old Testament became the Bible for many Jews, particularly for those living outside of Palestine. Most New Testament quotations of the Old Testament are from the Septuagint.

(3) Prophecies Concerning Egypt and Syria (11:5–20)

Verses 5–20 comprise a history of the ongoing conflicts between two divisions of the Greek Empire, the Ptolemaic (Egyptian) and the Seleucid (Syrian), from the death of Alexander (323 B.C.) until the reign of Antiochus IV (175–163 B.C.). The revelation was limited to these two divisions because Palestine, the home of God's people, lay between them and was continually involved in their later history. Originally a Ptolemaic territory, Palestine came under Seleucid control during the reign of Antiochus III (the "Great"). The stage was then set for the coming of the tyrant depicted in verses 21–35. In Dan. 11:5–35 "the king of the South" is an allusion to the Egyptian Pharaoh and "the king of the North" to the Seleucid (Syrian) leader.

(4) Prophecies Concerning Antiochus IV Epiphanes (11:21–35)

The historical information in verses 2–20 was furnished in order to introduce the Seleucid-Greek ruler, Antiochus IV Epiphanes (175–163 B.C.), the "little horn" of chapter 8 (see Dan. 8:9–12, 23–25). Much attention was given to this individual in the Book of Daniel because his actions profoundly affected Israel. The career of Antiochus may be divided as follows: accession to the throne and early reign (11:21–24), a further description of the first Egyptian war and subsequent Jewish persecution (11:25–28), the second Egyptian campaign (11:29–30a), and further persecutions of the Jews (11:30b–35).

Antiochus IV is labeled a "contemptible person" ("a despised person") by the Scripture writer because from the Jewish vantage point he was a monster. He persecuted the Jews, slaughtering thousands, and represented one of the greatest threats to the true religion in all of Israel's history. This arrogant monarch referred to himself as Epiphanes, the "Manifest One" or "Illustrious One"; but others called him Epimanes, the "Madman."

After his first Egyptian campaign (ca. 169 B.C.), Antiochus attacked Jerusalem ("holy covenant")

The Roman Ultimatum

As the Seleucid army was moving to besiege Alexandria, the Roman commander Gaius Popilius Laenas met Antiochus four miles outside of the city and handed him a letter from the Roman Senate ordering him to leave Egypt or face war with Rome. Then the Roman commander drew a circle in the sand around Antiochus and told him that he must respond before stepping from the circle. Well-aware of the might of Rome having been a hostage there and also remembering his father's (Antiochus III) defeat by the Roman legions at the Battle of Magnesia, the Syrian king stood in humiliated silence for a brief interval and then acquiesced to the demand.

and wreaked havoc on the Jewish people (v. 28). He massacred eighty thousand men, women, and children (2 Macc. 5:12–14) and then looted the Temple with the help of the evil high priest, Menelaus (see 2 Macc. 5:15–21). In 168 B.C. Antiochus invaded Egypt again, but this campaign did not turn out like the earlier one (v. 29). He encountered opposition from the "ships of the western coastlands [kittim]," that is, the Roman fleet that had come to Alexandria at the request of the Ptolemies (v. 30).

In 167 B.C. Antiochus vented "his fury" on the Jewish people once more (see 1 Macc. 1:29ff.; 2 Macc. 6:1ff.). On the Sabbath, the Syrian forces suddenly attacked, killing many people and plundering the city (see 1 Macc. 1:30–32; 2 Macc. 5:25–26). Antiochus's forces desecrated the Temple and abolished the daily sacrifice (v. 31).

Later in 167 B.C. the suppression of the Jewish religion began on a grand scale (1 Macc. 1:41ff.; 2 Macc. 6:1ff.). Jewish religious practices such as circumcision, possessing the Scriptures, sacrifices, and feast days were forbidden on penalty of death (1 Macc. 1:50, 63). Desecration of the Jewish religion reached its climax in December 167 B.C. (1 Macc. 1:54) when an altar or idol-statue to Olympian Zeus (Jupiter) was erected in the Temple ("the abomination that causes desolation"), and ten days later sacrifices, probably including swine (see 1 Macc. 1:47; 2 Macc. 6:4–5), were offered on the altar (see 1 Macc. 1:54, 59).

Yet even in this dark period, there were true believers among the Jews who remained faithful to their God (v. 32; see 1 Macc. 1:62–63). Foremost among those who resisted the oppressive

The Maccabean Martyrs

The Letter to the Hebrews seems to refer to some of the faithful heroes from the Maccabean period. "Who became powerful in battle and routed foreign armies" (Heb. 11:34) evidently points to the victories of the Maccabean forces. "Others were tortured and refused to be released, so that they might gain a better resurrection" (Heb. 11:35) probably speaks of the martyrdom of a mother and her seven sons who were horribly tortured and then burned (cf. 2 Macc. 7:1–41).

measures of Antiochus were the Maccabees, the family of a certain priest named Mattathias (1 Macc. 2:1ff.). He had five sons John, Simon, Judas, Eleazar, and Jonathan, three of whom (Judas, Jonathan, and Simon) became known as the Maccabees, although the term *Maccabeus* ("hammer") originally was given only to Judas (1 Macc. 2:4). The Maccabees overthrew the Syrian yoke through a series of brilliant military victories against Antiochus's military commanders, Apollonius, Seron, Gorgias, and Lysias (1 Macc. 3:10–4:35) between 166 (or 165) and 164 B.C., and as a result the temple was rededicated to the Lord on December 14, 164 B.C. (1 Macc. 4:52). Verses 33–35 refer to true believers ("wise") who would remain faithful in spite of persecution.

"A little help" (v. 34) is the Maccabean revolt that grew and eventually threw off the Syrian yoke. The purpose of Israel's fiery ordeal was to cleanse individuals and the nation as a whole of sinful practices and strengthen their faith. Antiochus IV died in 163 B.C. during an expedition in Persia (1 Macc. 6:1–16; 2 Macc. 9:1–29), bringing to an "end" both his wicked life and his atrocities against God's people.

■ *God gave these prophecies of the future to*
■ *His people as an encouragement to faithful-*
■ *ness when the crisis arrived. Prophecy of*
■ *events in the last days is a summons to*
■ *be prepared.*

Theological Value of Daniel 11:2–35

This section of the Book of Daniel is not merely an unimportant record of past historical events, but a rich testimony to the believer's glorious God and the trustworthiness of His Word. First, the reality and omniscience of the God of the Bible is demonstrated here. In the first thirty-five verses one scholar has counted 135 prophecies that have already been fulfilled and can be documented by a study of the history of the period. Second, for those who live after the predicted events have occurred, there is the confidence that since the previous prophecies have been fulfilled, the subsequent promises of deliverance and triumph will just as assuredly come true. Third, the fulfillment of these amazing predictions shows that the Holy Scriptures are a product of supernatural revelation.

Daniel predicted that this king would "come to his end" in Palestine (v. 45), but it is a matter of historical record that Antiochus IV died at Tabae in Persia.

(5) Prophecies Concerning the End-times (11:36–12:3)

Some scholars hold that 11:36–12:3 continues to speak of the life and times of Antiochus IV. However, much of the historical data set forth in this section is impossible to harmonize with Antiochus's life. For example, Antiochus did not exalt himself above every god (vv. 36–37), reject "the gods of his fathers" (v. 37), or worship "a god unknown to his fathers" (v. 38); on the contrary, he worshiped the Greek pantheon, even building an altar and offering sacrifices to Zeus in the Jerusalem Temple precincts.

The context indicates that this ruler would live in the last days, immediately prior to the coming of the Lord. Verse 40 reveals that this king's activities would take place "at the time of the end" (see Dan. 10:14), and the resurrection of the saints would occur immediately after God delivers His people from this evil individual's power (see 12:2). Daniel previously has described this person (e.g., 7:8, 11, 20–22, 24–26) and expected the reader to recognize him without an introduction. He is the eschatological Antichrist, a view widely accepted since early times (e.g., Jerome in the fourth century A.D.).

THE KING'S EVIL CHARACTER (11:36–39)

In verses 36–39 the Antichrist is described as arrogant, blasphemous (see 7:8, 11, 20, 25; 2 Thess. 2:4; Rev. 13:5–6), successful, atheistic (2 Thess. 2:4; Rev. 13:6), and militaristic. He will be successful until God's wrath ("the time of wrath"; v. 36) is poured out on him and the whole sinful world in the last days (Dan. 12:1; Rev. 6–19).

"The one desired by women" (v. 37) could mean "that desired by women," "the one desired by women," or even "the desire for women." Sometimes the phrase has been interpreted as a reference to Christ since Jewish women desired to be the mother of the Messiah. The context of the verse seems to support that interpretation. On either side of the phrase, there are statements concerning the Antichrist's contempt for God and religion. It would not be surprising to find a reference to the rejection of the Messiah in this setting. Rather than worshiping God, Antichrist will honor military power ("god of fortresses," v. 38). That Antichrist will engage in war is affirmed in verses 40–45; 7:8, 24; and elsewhere in Scripture (e.g., Rev. 13:4; 16:13–16).

THE KING'S WARS DESCRIBED (11:40–45)

A great battle is described in verses 40–45, and the time of this conflict is declared to be "the time of the end" (v. 40). This battle would conclude with the destruction of the Antichrist in Palestine (v. 45), followed by the resurrection of the saints (12:2).

"The king of the South" will attack the "king of the North," who will retaliate. "Chariots and cavalry and a great fleet of ships" would be representative of their modern counterparts. It seems clear from the description of the "king of the North" that he is Antichrist, but the identification of the "king of the South" is a matter of conjecture. Since "the South" earlier in the chapter referred to Egypt, the reference may be to a confederacy of powers led by Egypt or including Egypt.

The Antichrist "will invade" the "countries" of those who have attacked him and will "sweep through them like a flood." He "will also invade" Israel, "the Beautiful Land" (v. 41; cp. 8:9; 11:16). "Many countries will fall" to this powerful ruler. For some unknown reason, "Edom, Moab and the leaders of Ammon" (modern Jordan) would be spared his fury, but Egypt, Libya, and the Nubians (modern Ethiopia and Sudan) would be conquered by him (vv. 42–43).

While subjugating the southern regions (where the attack against him seems to have originated), the Antichrist will receive "reports from the east and the north" that "alarm him" (v. 44). Evidently he will hear that new attacks have been launched against his interests from nations in the east (possibly the armies described in Rev. 9:13–19; 16:12) and the north (possibly the invasion from the north prophesied in Ezek. 38–39). Furious that anyone would dare oppose his power and authority, the evil dictator will marshal his forces against the enemy with the intent of obliterating them.

Antichrist will meet these attacking forces in Palestine and make his headquarters "between the seas at the beautiful holy mountain" (v. 45). "Seas" denotes the two great bodies of water on either side of Israel, the Mediterranean Sea on the west and the Dead Sea on the east. The "beautiful holy mountain" is Mount Zion where the Temple stood, rendering the mountain "beautiful" and "holy." Antichrist will use the Jerusalem Temple for his headquarters (see 2 Thess. 2:4; possibly Matt. 24:15), although the brunt of the battle will be elsewhere. Daniel reported that the final war will be fought in Israel, a fact set forth elsewhere in Scripture (Ezek. 39:2–29; Joel 3:2–16; Zech. 12:2–9; 14:1–21). The Book of Revelation indicates more specifically that the valley of Megiddo will be the setting of this final conflict—the battle of Armageddon (Rev. 16:16).

Now the great deliverance of the saints alluded to in 12:1 is explained. Antichrist, the great persecutor of God's people, "will come to his end, and no one will help him." Finally, the career of the most evil man in history will be terminated. Daniel revealed earlier in the book that "the little horn" will be judged when the Lord comes to set up His kingdom (7:11, 26, 27; cp. 2 Thess. 2:8; Rev. 19:20).

DANIEL 12

The Final Triumph and Reward of God's People (12:1–3)

In spite of the chapter division found in both the English and Hebrew Bibles, Daniel's final vision continues without interruption from 11:45 through 12:3. The closing verses of Dan. 11 describe the Antichrist's military and political career, whereas his internal policy of unparalleled oppression and persecution of God's people is set forth in 12:1. Verse 1 also relates the final deliverance of the saints, followed in verses 2–3 by an account of their glorious condition in the Messianic kingdom.

"At that time" (12:1) alludes to the period just described in 11:36–45—Antichrist's reign of terror at "the time of the end" (11:40). God has assigned Michael to protect Daniel's people (see Rev. 12:7–9). Michael's help will be needed because Israel will experience "a time of distress" (Matt. 24:21) unlike anything the world has ever known. Yet the Jewish remnant (and all other persons) who trust in the Lord

"The Book"

The "book" (12:1) is a common biblical figure and alludes to the "book of life" in which the names of all saints are written (see Exod. 32:33; Ps. 69:28; Mal. 3:16; Luke 10:20; Rev. 3:5; 20:12). Evidently, this symbol comes from the practice of keeping a record of all the citizens of a town. Those whose names were listed enjoyed the blessings of community membership, whereas the names of those who were excommunicated from fellowship were blotted out.

will ultimately "be delivered" from Antichrist's oppression.

One of the most blessed truths in Scripture—the resurrection—is set forth in verse 2. After the "time of distress" described in the previous verses, "multitudes" will be raised from the grave. "Sleep" is a figure of speech used frequently in the Bible to designate physical death (see John 11:11–14; Acts 7:60; 1 Thess. 4:13; 1 Cor. 15:51), and it should be emphasized that this "sleep" refers to physical death *only*. When the spirit of the believer leaves the body, it goes directly into the presence of the Lord (see 2 Cor. 5:8; Phil. 1:21–23). Daniel 12:2 lends no support to the theories of some groups that persons who die are annihilated or experience "soul sleep."

Although the spirit of the believer does not sleep, the body is placed in a grave ("the dust of the earth"; see Gen. 3:19) and becomes inactive (sleeps) until the Lord raises it, glorifies it, and reunites it with the spirit (1 Cor. 15:51–55). Deceased unbelievers will also be resurrected and spend eternity in bodily form, according to this verse (see Matt. 10:28). The resurrection of the body is compared here to a person waking from sleep.

Two groups of resurrected persons with drastically different futures are represented in verse 2 (see John 5:28–29), and the fate of both groups is "everlasting." Believers will rise to enjoy "everlasting life" in their new bodies and will reign with Christ (Rev. 20:4–6). Here the phrase, "everlasting life," appears for the first time in the Old Testament. Daniel related that there will be "multitudes" of resurrected believers, although this does not necessarily mean they will be the majority of the human race (Matt. 7:13–14). On the other hand, unbelievers will face "shame and everlasting contempt." The wicked will be ashamed and disgraced as they stand before the Lord and realize the gravity of their sin.

Daniel 12:2 is generally considered to contain the most explicit reference in the Old Testament to the resurrection of the individual, but other Old Testament passages teach this doctrine as well (see Job 19:26; Ps. 17:15; Isa. 26:19). Revelation 20:4–6 seems to indicate that the resurrection of the saints after the tribulation period (the group described here) and the resurrection of the wicked will be separated by a thousand years. As is the case with other Old Testament prophecies (see Zech. 9:9–10), future events separated by many years are sometimes telescoped together with later revelation clarifying the time difference.

THE RESURRECTION

A number of truths concerning the resurrection are set forth in this passage. First, it is a bodily resurrection. The body is brought out of the grave and infused with new life. Second, this new body is immortal. Third, even unbelievers will spend eternity in bodily form. Fourth, the resurrected saints receive great honor and great reward, whereas the opposite is true for unbelievers.

In the Messianic age, believers ("wise") will be greatly honored ("shine like the brightness of the heavens . . . like the stars," v. 3; cp. 8:10).

"Contempt"

The Hebrew word translated "contempt" refers to "an object of aversion" or "abhorrence." In Isaiah 66:24, the only other instance of this word in the Old Testament, it also concerns the eternal state: "And they will go out and look upon the dead bodies of those who rebelled against me; their worm will not die, nor will their fire be quenched, and they will be *loathsome* to all mankind." Isaiah's use of the term *loathsome* appears to explain the significance of the expression in Daniel 12:2. So shocking will be the fate of the lost that onlookers must turn their faces away in horror (or disgust). This "contempt" will be "everlasting,"—it will endure for eternity.

Daniel 12:3 in the New Testament

Christ, evidently with Dan. 12:3 in mind, declared that at the end of the age, "the righteous will shine like the sun in the kingdom of their Father" (Matt. 13:43). Paul appears to have used phraseology from this passage in Phil. 2:15.

■ *An evil king will rise to power in the end*
■ *times who will fight great wars and persecute*
■ *the saints. But the Lord will judge him and*
■ *deliver His people. The saints will be resur-*
■ *rected and take part in a wonderful new*
■ *world where they will be honored.*

QUESTIONS TO GUIDE YOUR STUDY

1. What is the purpose of the historical pre-view of 11:2–20?

2. Who is the subject of 11:21–35?

3. Who is the king of 11:36–45? Describe his character and his career.

4. What does 12:2 teach concerning the res-urrection of the dead?

5. What will it be like for the saints in the Messianic age?

Seal the Scroll

In the ancient Near East, the custom was to "seal" (12:4) an important document by impressing upon it the identifying marks of the parties involved and the recording scribe. The original document was duplicated and placed ("closed up") in a safe place where it could be preserved. There was also an unsealed copy of the deed that was presumably open for inspection. An excellent illustration of this process is recorded in the Book of Jeremiah (Jer. 32:9–12).

4. Final Instructions to Daniel (12:4–13)

With 12:3 the vision proper ends. The remain-der of the book contains the admonition to pre-serve the prophecy, information concerning the duration of history's final phase, and various personal remarks and promises to Daniel.

(1) Instructions to Preserve the Message (12:4)

Gabriel instructed Daniel to preserve ("seal"; cp. 8:26) the scroll, not merely this final vision, but the whole book for those who will live at "the time of the end." This future generation will undergo the horrors of the "time of distress" (cp. 12:1) and will need the precious promises con-tained in the Book of Daniel—that God will be victorious over the kingdoms of this world and that the suffering will last for only a brief time.

An increase in travel toward the end of the age is not the idea of the phrase, "will go here and there." In a number of Old Testament passages (see 2 Chron. 16:9; Jer. 5:1; Amos 8:12; Zech. 4:10), the Hebrew word denotes "to go here and there" in search of a person or thing. The purpose of this search will be "to increase knowledge." Yet Gabriel was not predicting a mere surge in scientific "knowledge" in the last days. A particular kind of "knowledge" was intended—when and how Daniel's message would be fulfilled. As the time of fulfillment draws nearer, the "wise" will seek to comprehend these prophecies more precisely, and God will grant understanding ("knowledge") to them.

(2) Duration of the "Time of Distress" (12:5–7)

Daniel 12:5–13 serves as a conclusion to the whole book as well as to chapters 10–12. Two additional angels, standing on opposite banks of the Tigris River (see Dan. 10:4), suddenly appeared to Daniel (v. 5).

At this point in the narrative "the man clothed in linen" (Christ; cp. 10:5–6) is reintroduced. He is described as standing in mid-air "above the waters of the river." Gabriel's question (v. 6) to "the man clothed in linen" is not, How long will it be before these things take place? but, How long will they continue when they begin to occur? Such an understanding is confirmed by the reply in the next verse. In 8:13 the exact Hebrew phrase translated "how long" was also employed to describe the duration of a predicted crisis. "Astonishing things" will occur during this period—the evil career of the Antichrist, the great war, and the "time of distress."

"The man clothed in linen" responded to the angel's question by raising both hands toward heaven and swearing by the authority of God Himself that this period would last "for a time, times and half a time." Raising the hand in an oath was the usual practice (see Gen. 14:22; Deut. 32:40; Rev. 10:5–6), but raising both hands and swearing to keep the oath in the name of the eternal God offered the greatest possible assurance that the words spoken are true.

Christ in the Book of Daniel

Christ's Kingdom	2:34–35, 44–45
Fourth Man in the Furnace	3:25, 28
Daniel's Protector from the Lions	6:22
Son of Man	7:13–14, 27
One Who Looked like a Man	8:15–17
Anointed One, the Ruler	9:25–26
Man Dressed in Linen	10:4–6; 12:6–7

The phrase, "a time, times and half a time," is the duration of the period (see Dan. 7:25; also 4:16, 25, 32). As in 7:25, the tribulation will last three and a half years, the time corresponding to the second half of the "seven" mentioned in 9:27. Thus, the sovereign Lord of the universe is promising directly and emphatically that the Antichrist's horrors (the "time of distress" of

12:1) perpetrated on God's people and the whole world will last only a brief time. Saints of the tribulation period may count on the verity of this pledge.

During this time, Israel will be defeated by their enemies ("power . . . broken"). That the Jewish state will be attacked by many nations and crushed by them is taught elsewhere in Scripture (see Zech. 12–14). When in desperate straits, the Jewish people will cry out to God for help, repent of their sins, and receive Jesus as their Messiah (see Zech. 12:10–14). At that time the Lord will return to rule the earth, and the tribulation will end (Zech. 14:3–11).

(3) Daniel's Question and the Reply (12:8–13)

Daniel desired to know, "What will the outcome of all this be?" (v. 8). "All this" includes the whole range of end-time events that the angel had revealed to Daniel in this vision—the Antichrist's activities, the tribulation, as well as Israel's persecution and deliverance. The question concerning "the outcome of all this" may mean, What would happen at the end of these things? or possibly, How would these things be brought to an end?

Purpose of Trials

Although they will intensify in the last days, believers have endured trials throughout the history of the church. Afflictions have tended to make believers more holy (12:10).

Gabriel (or "the man clothed in linen") tactfully replied, "Go your way, Daniel" (v. 9). This was not a rebuke (additional information is provided in vv. 11–12) but simply indicated that the prophet should go on about his life and not be concerned about his lack of knowledge because the vision related to the distant future. Yet Daniel was assured that these prophecies would be preserved ("closed up and sealed"; cp. v. 4) for those who would need them at "the time of the end." Then "knowledge" concerning the vision would be given to the saints (cp. v. 4). As the end approaches, the messages of Daniel (and other prophecies of the last days) will become increasingly clearer to believers.

The time when "many will be purified, made spotless and refined" is the "time of distress" in the last days (v. 10). Although the saints will be purified, "the wicked will continue to be wicked." That many people undergoing the horrors of the tribulation will still refuse to repent and be saved is repeated several times in the Book of Revelation (9:20–21; 16:9, 11). Even the chaos and calamities of the last days will not bring some persons to recognize ("understand") their need for God.

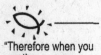

"Therefore when you see the ABOMINATION OF DESOLATION which was spoken of through Daniel the prophet, standing in the holy place (let the reader understand), then let those who are in Judea flee to the mountains."

Matthew 24:15–16, NASB

The "time of distress" will begin when the Antichrist abolishes worship (see Dan. 9:27) and sets up "the abomination that causes desolation" (v. 11; cp. Matt. 24:15). The exact nature of the Antichrist's "abomination" is unclear, but it is evidently some idolatrous object (see Dan. 11:31). Its presence in the Temple will cause believers to cease worshipping there and thus render the Temple desolate, that is, empty of worshipers.

In 12:6–7 Daniel revealed that the great tribulation will last for three and one-half years (approximately 1,260 days in round numbers, figuring thirty days per month). The text states that 1,290 days will transpire from the time the Antichrist begins his persecution until some unspecified event thirty days after the tribulation ends. Most likely the extra days will be the time in which the nations are judged by the Lord immediately following His return (see Matt. 25:31–46). Then a special blessing was pronounced on those who reach the end of

1,335 days (v. 12). An additional forty-five days was appended to the 1,290 days. Dogmatism is not proper, but it has been reasonably suggested that this date is the official inauguration of Christ's reign.

God had revealed many wonderful truths to Daniel over the years, but verse 13 implies that no more revelations would be granted him. The prophet was now a very old man, and he was instructed to stop being anxious concerning these matters and to be satisfied with what he had been told for as long as he lives ("go your way till the end"). Daniel would die (probably soon after this vision) and "rest" from the labors of this life, but "at the end of the days" he would be resurrected (see Dan. 12:2) and "receive" his reward. These precious promises of resurrection and reward are not limited to Daniel but pertain to all the "wise" who have placed their faith in the Messiah, the Lord Jesus, and will someday "shine like the brightness of the heavens" and "like the stars for ever and ever!"

■ *Daniel's prophecy concluded on a very posi-*
■ *tive note. God's message to Daniel will be*
■ *preserved as a comfort to the saints in the*
■ *future. A difficult time will come, but its*
■ *duration will be brief. Then a blessed period*
■ *of history will begin. Daniel (and other*
■ *saints) will be resurrected and take part in*
■ *this wonderful age.*

QUESTIONS TO GUIDE YOUR STUDY

1. What do the words "close up and seal the words" mean?
2. What kind of "knowledge" does Daniel indicate people will seek in the last days?
3. What is the duration of the "time of distress"? How did the "man clothed in linen" emphasize the certainty of His pronouncement?
4. What promise did God make to Daniel in the prophecy's last verse?

REFERENCE SOURCES USED

Archer, Gleason L., Jr. *Daniel*. Expositor's Bible Commentary. Grand Rapids: Zondervan, 1985.

Baldwin, Joyce G. *Daniel*. Tyndale Old Testament Commentaries. Downers Grove: InterVarsity, 1978.

Boice, James Montgomery. *Daniel: An Expositional Commentary*. Grand Rapids: Zondervan, 1989.

Butler, Trent C., ed. *Holman Bible Dictionary*. Nashville: Holman, 1991.

Criswell, W. A. *Expository Sermons on the Book of Daniel*. Grand Rapids: Zondervan, 1976.

Dockery, David S., ed. *Holman Bible Handbook*. Nashville: Holman, 1992.

Keil, C. F. *Biblical Commentary on the Book of Daniel*. Grand Rapids: Eerdmans, 1973.

Leupold, H. C. *Exposition of Daniel*. Grand Rapids: Baker, 1969.

Miller, Stephen R. *Daniel*. New American Commentary. Nashville: Broadman and Holman, 1994.

Phillips, John and Jerry Vines. *Exploring the Book of Daniel*. Neptune, N.J.: Loizeaux, 1990.

Walvoord, John. F. *Daniel: The Key to Prophetic Revelation*. Chicago: Moody, 1971.

Whitcomb, John C. *Daniel*. Chicago: Moody, 1985.

Wood, Leon. *A Survey of Israel's History*. Rev. David O'Brien. Grand Rapids: Zondervan, 1986.

Young, Edward J. *The Prophecy of Daniel*. Grand Rapids: Eerdmans, 1949.